Librarian's Guide to Passive Programming

Librarian's Guide to Passive Programming

Easy and Affordable Activities for All Ages

Emily T. Wichman

LIBRARIES UNLIMITED

AN IMPRINT OF ABC-CLIO, LLC
Santa Barbara, California • Denver, Colorado • Oxford, England

Copyright 2012 by ABC-CLIO, LLC

Library of Congress Cataloging-in-Publication Data

Wichman, Emily T.
  Librarian's guide to passive programming : easy and affordable activities for all ages / Emily T.
  Wichman.
     pages cm
  Includes bibliographical references and index.
    ISBN 978–1–59884–895–3 (pbk.) — ISBN 978–1–59884–896–0 (ebook) (print) 1. Libraries—Activity
programs—United States. I. Title.
Z716.33.W53   2012
025.5—dc23   2011045419

ISBN: 978–1–59884–895–3
EISBN: 978–1–59884–896–0

16 15 14 13 12   1 2 3 4 5

This book is also available on the World Wide Web as an eBook.
Visit www.abc-clio.com for details.

Libraries Unlimited
An Imprint of ABC-CLIO, LLC

ABC-CLIO, LLC
130 Cremona Drive, P.O. Box 1911
Santa Barbara, California 93116-1911

This book is printed on acid-free paper ∞

Manufactured in the United States of America

For Mom and Dad

Contents

Acknowledgments

When I began this project, I knew that my best bet for locating librarians willing to discuss passive programming was to post on library listservs. The communities at PUBYAC, PUBLIB, Fiction_L, and LM_NET are full of wonderful people who are dedicated professionals. When I sent out inquiries about passive programming, dozens of you responded. Some had never done programming of this type but offered words of encouragement. I offer you my appreciation and admiration.

Those who shared with me programs that are featured in this book are acknowledged by name and library throughout the text. Each of you took time out of your busy lives to describe your programs in detail, share program materials, and answer my numerous questions. This book couldn't have been written without you. I am in your debt and I know that your creativity will inspire everyone who reads about your programs.

To my coworkers past and present at the Milford-Miami Township Branch of Clermont County Public Library, I give my thanks. Working with you is a pleasure. Other departments deserving of my gratitude include: Administration for support, the Office of Public Affairs and Programs for ideas, and Multimedia Resources for graphics.

Introduction

Passive Programming: What Is It and Why Should You Care?

The traditional library program takes place at a set time, on a specific day, most often in the library's meeting room. The program might be a book club, a puppet show, a local history lecture, a storytime, a computer class, or any of the other countless presentations and activities that take place daily in libraries. While these programs can be a wonderful experience for both the public and staff, they come with their share of frustrations. What if there's severe weather on program day? What if the program was unwittingly scheduled to conflict with the school carnival? What if a co-worker calls in sick, who will cover the desk during the program?

Passive programs neatly sidestep these concerns by taking place over an extended period of time and by being available for patrons to participate in anytime the library is open. These programs might even take place entirely online. Passive programs can be built around almost any topic, typically cost little to implement, and require only minimal staff involvement beyond initial setup and ongoing promotion. Such programs can be thought of as self-directed, self-serve, or do-it-yourself activities for library users to participate in at their own pace and convenience.

Passive programs aren't a replacement for traditional library programs; instead, they should be thought of as a supplement to your programming repertoire. Libraries across the country are facing budget cuts and are being forced to reduce services. Passive programs are generally inexpensive in terms of both supply and staff costs, making them perfect for cash-strapped libraries. These programs eliminate scheduling conflicts, because they can be planned and implemented at your leisure. Often the prep work can be done during a slow desk shift. Has your library been hesitant to involve volunteers in programming? Passive programs are an easy way to incorporate volunteers; because their interaction with the public is limited, less training is required. Volunteers can assist in preparing supplies and monitoring the active program.

Even in times of plenty, passive programs are desirable because they encourage patrons to linger in the library. Passive programs can be used to highlight parts of the collection, showcase library services, and complement community initiatives. Often taking place over the span of a month, these activities allow patrons to customize their interaction with the library. Our users' lives are full with families, jobs, household chores, hobbies, and dozens of other things. Competition for the public's time and attention is fierce, and distractions are numerous. Make it easy for your patrons to participate in a library program, while easing the burden on your library's resources, by launching a few passive programs of your own.

Developing Ideas for Passive Programs

This book provides you with 32 different passive program plans, along with many suggestions on how to modify the programs for alternate variations. Passive programs can be taken in many directions, and the process for choosing suitable topics is similar to the approach taken for developing traditional programs. Sources of inspiration are numerous:

- Colleagues—Swap ideas with other programmers. Monitor listservs. Consider a traditional program that has been successful and think of a way to build a passive program around its theme.

- Current services—Some library services lend themselves to passive programming. The Laid-Back Book Club is a book club without formal meetings. The Spreading Cheer Project creates items to be distributed during senior outreach. The Literary Gnome is a source of passive readers' advisory.

- Promote collections and services—A book display can be tied in to almost any passive program. Want to spotlight the knitting, crocheting, and sewing books? Host a Crafting for Charity event. Want people to take notice of underused resources? Scavenger hunts are a great way to direct people to specific features of the library.

- Monitor patron interests—What materials circulate most heavily? What topics come up repeatedly at the reference desk? Consider these themes when brainstorming program ideas.

- Spinoff major library initiatives—When collecting programs for this book, I found time and again libraries offering passive programs in conjunction with their summer reading programs. Community reading projects, major anniversaries, and national celebrations such as Teen Read Week are prime opportunities for passive programming.

- Community building—Think of ways to get library users interacting with each other. Exchange programs are a great way to swap resources. Group writing projects allow for shared creativity. Do You Recognize Me? taps the collective memory to identify historic photographs, while '80s Month gets visitors reminiscing.

- Community happenings—Is there a new exhibit opening at the museum? What musical will be performed at the theater? Which festival is just around the corner? What topics have been big in the news? Tie passive programs into these events.

- Local organizations—Want to establish or expand upon a relationship with a local organization? Think about its services and how they might be featured in a passive program.

- School curriculums—Partner with local schools by planning passive programs that complement topics taught in class.

- Skills development—Design a program to help participants learn or improve a specific skill. The Shredded Book Contest encourages patrons to use the catalog. Letterboxing at the Library helps children with counting skills and learning to follow directions.

Supplies for Passive Programming

Most passive programs don't require a lot of supplies beyond items the typical library already has on hand, in addition to the occasional prize. Limited materials consumption, in conjunction with the fact that you'll never find yourself hiring a performer for a passive program, is a big part of what makes this type of programming so efficient. Programs that involve a craft can be an exception, but ample opportunities exist for using recycled materials and leftover supplies. Since craft programs practically guarantee high participation levels, cost per participant rates tend to be reasonable.

For each program plan, I only provide a supply list if unique items are required. The materials on these lists are things that the average library might not have readily available. Many of the programs require only very general supplies. If your library lacks any of the items listed below, I recommend trying to obtain them. I can guarantee that these supplies are things you'll find useful in endeavors beyond passive programming.

- Basic office supplies—markers, tape, scissors, stapler, etc.

- Basic office equipment—computer, printer, digital camera, paper cutter

- Colored paper—Both copier-weight and cardstock can be useful.

- Large roll of white paper—This paper can be used for making posters and covering activity tables.

- Roll of perforated tickets

- Pens or pencils—Many passive programs require completing an entry form. Purchase inexpensive writing implements, as you will surely lose some.

- Pencil cup

- Easels—Both tabletop and floor styles are helpful.

- Book stands

- Acrylic sign holders—A variety of sizes in both horizontal and vertical orientations will come in handy.

- Acrylic display boxes—Use these for displaying prizes and adding height to program displays.

- Entry box

Marketing Passive Programs

Because passive programs are so easy to do, the temptation is there to pull them together at the last minute or create them the moment a good idea strikes. While this rushed approach might occasionally be appropriate, particularly when tying a program in to a timely issue, I generally recommend that you plan passive programs with the same timeline you would use for traditional programs. Advance planning allows for better marketing. Just because a passive program might be easy and inexpensive doesn't mean you should skimp on publicity. Passive programs aren't second class. If you're going to put in the time to create something special for your patrons, then insist that your program get the full marketing treatment that your library normally provides for a traditional program. Promote the program through posters, newsletters, press releases, online, and any other outlets used by your library. If partnering with another organization on your passive program, be sure that they're promoting the program also.

How you chose to execute the program impacts its success. If your library is part of a multiple-branch system, why not hold the program simultaneously at all locations? Promotion is more efficient and the cost of reproducing the program at another location is less than creating additional programs from scratch. Can you run the program online while simultaneously conducting it in the library building? Programs like Celebrity Encounters, Crazy Captions, Get a Clue, Mr. Gnome Reads the Classics, Mystery Theme Contest, and Name That Story lend themselves perfectly to this dual format. For programs held in the library, positioning is essential. Set up the program in a high-traffic area, either near the entrance, the service desk, or in an area frequented by the target audience. Don't let the program get lost in the clutter. Set up your display on a table, a countertop, or a piece of display furniture. An appropriately decorated bulletin board makes the perfect backdrop for many activities.

Passive programs lend themselves to cross-promotion. As suggested previously, tie in a passive program with a traditional program or major celebration. Display items from the library's collection that relate to the theme of the program. Use open space near the setup to display materials about new or underused library services.

Often, the ultimate key to a successful program is talking about it. Make sure all staff members are aware of the program. They need to know what the program is, how long it runs, where it is set up, and details on how to participate. This is particularly important for frontline staff. The people at the circulation desk are a major source of promotion potential. Passive programs are perfect for people who are waiting. You have a ready audience in parents waiting for children to complete a homework assignment, kids waiting to be picked up, people waiting to get on a computer, tutors waiting to meet with students, people who arrive early to attend a traditional program, new patrons having library cards made, and borrowers waiting for you to locate an item missing from the shelves. Provide these patrons with something worthwhile to do while they wait. They can be your next passive program participants!

Evaluating the Success of Passive Programs

Tracking attendance is an important tool in judging the success of a program. With traditional programs, determining attendance is often simply a matter of counting how many people walk in the door. Since the primary purpose of passive programming is to provide activities that patrons can participate in at their leisure, counting attendance can prove more difficult. There are a few different techniques that can be used to track participation. Be sure to design at least one into your passive program and you'll have a mechanism for gauging its success. Depending upon the circumstances, some of the techniques are more effective than others.

1. Requiring patrons to complete an answer sheet as part of the program is the easiest and most accurate way of tracking participation. If the person finished the program, he or she completed an answer sheet. All you have to do is open the entry box and count.

2. Design the program so that patrons must see a staff member in order to participate. With a craft program, this might involve keeping a potentially high-loss supply behind the service desk. For a program in which space or supplies are limited, such as the LEGO Display, require participants to register. Programs such as Letterboxing at the Library make interacting with staff part of the activity.

3. If a program requires patrons to consume supplies, you can record the quantity of materials you put out, and then subtract the number that remain at the end of the program to determine participation. This technique works particularly well with craft programs. The downside of this method is that you can't track unique participants or know for certain that all supplies were used for the intended purpose.

4. Offering a prize can provide strong incentive for participation. If the program does not include an answer sheet, then participants need to be provided with an entry ticket. A good prize should spur people to come to the desk for their entry tickets, but I have often been surprised by how many people will participate in a program and then forego the entry ticket. Whether this is done intentionally is hard to determine.

Once you have attendance numbers, how do you know if passive programming is a success? Consider doing a cost analysis of your programming efforts. Add up staff, supply, publicity, and any other costs. Use these figures to determine the true cost of the program per participant. Compare several passive programs to several traditional programs. Are the costs comparable? Which programs have the lowest cost per participant? These figures will guide you in making future programming decisions.

Of course, the success of a program can't be solely measured in how many people attend or how inexpensive it is to pull off. Any program has the potential to yield positive impacts, many of which are difficult to measure quantitatively. Did a program prompt a participant to explore a new part of the library's collection? Did that person check out a display book that might have otherwise remained undiscovered? Did patrons learn about a library service, maybe using it themselves or referring it to friends? Did a person discover a new area of interest, get inspired to try a new hobby, or improve a skill? Was a partnership with a community agency strengthened? If you're lucky, program participants will share these benefits with you, but as with many other library services, you have to resign yourself to the fact that you will never know the full impact of your efforts. What you can do is plan your programs with these outcomes in mind, using statistics and feedback as a guide, and trust that you are helping to further the mission of the library.

Scope and Organization

This book contains passive programs that are suitable for all ages: children, teens, and adults. Many are intended for an intergenerational audience, designed to intrigue both children and adults and to create opportunities for families to participate together in the activities. Some programs originally designed for one age group, such as Name That Story or the Shredded Book Contest, can be modified to appeal to another.

Many of the program plans presented were designed by me. The library I am employed with, Clermont County Public Library (OH), has a long history of passive programming and is where I first became familiar with the practice. My coworkers have contributed some of the programs and resources contained here. Other programs were graciously shared by fellow library workers, whom I met through online means and who are acknowledged in each program plan.

The programs featured in this book meet the criteria of my passive programming definition. While large-scale reading programs such as summer reading are technically passive programs, these generally require significant expenditures of both supplies and staff time and have not be included. Entire books can and have been devoted solely to these types of programs. In speaking with librarians across the country, the one type of passive program that seems to be extremely common is the coloring table or craft table. Intended for young children and typically positioned in the Children's Department, these are tables laid out with coloring sheets and crayons or sometimes simple crafts. Due to their familiarity and straightforward nature, I do not discuss this standard program type further in this book.

Another style of program encountered with some regularity is the "make and take" activity. These are prepared crafts or activity booklets that patrons take home to complete at their own pace. While "make and takes" can be considered passive programs, I have not included activities of this type due to my belief in the importance of passive programming as a promoter of lingering, either in the library or on the library's website. This lingering allows participants to connect with the library's collections, its services, and the community, and the value of passive programming lies in the outcomes that result from this engagement.

The programs presented in this book are grouped thematically into chapters. Supplemental materials, such as promotional items, handouts, and photographs, are included with each program to serve as models for your own preparations. Each program plan includes most, if not all, of the sections defined below.

- Description—A brief overview of the program.

- Supplies—Items required for the program that are beyond the scope of standard supplies typically available in libraries.

- Make It Happen—A list of steps that need to be taken in order to set up and run the program.

- Evaluation—Instructions on how to track participation in the program.

- Collection Tie-In—Suggestions for displaying library materials appropriate to the program. Display ideas are general subject areas or material types, as opposed to specific titles.

- Alternative Approaches—Ideas on how the program can be modified or reinvented. Some programs can be tweaked to run on a library's website.

- Resources—A list of helpful books or online resources.

Chapter 1

Books and Reading

This initial chapter has more programs than any other, which makes sense because libraries, at their core, are still very much about books. While some of our patrons visit only to use computers, or the meeting room, or to research a specific problem, it's safe to say that a significant portion of library users are also book lovers. The programs in this chapter acknowledge and celebrate that shared interest. You'll find programs based on the physical nature and appearance of books. Mr. Gnome Reads the Classics has participants identifying books by a portion of the cover art. Name That Story challenges participants to identify book titles from visual clues. The Shredded Book Contest literally asks patrons to see if they can identify a book from its very small parts. Other programs, such as the Laid-Back Book Club and The Literary Gnome, encourage discussion about books and the discovery of new titles. Use passive programs to feature authors. Library users try to identify bestselling authors by the first lines of their books in Guess the Author. Our Books Go Far gives a nod to the simple pleasure of leisure reading by encouraging patrons to share their vacation reads. The best part about reading-themed passive programs is the opportunity to promote your collection. Any book display can be livened up with an activity. Think about the theme, no matter what it is, and I bet you can come up with a passive program to accompany it. The possibilities are endless!

Guess the Author

All books begin in their own special way, but some are certainly more memorable than others. A good opening line will make you laugh, make you think, or maybe even make you pause; but above all, it will make you eager to read all of the lines that follow. The ability to craft an intriguing opener is an art that deserves to be celebrated. While the literati sometimes scoff at those authors who repeatedly top the *New York Times* bestseller lists, these writers certainly deserve credit for their engaging writing styles that pull readers in again and again. Just how familiar are library patrons with those bestselling authors? Test reader knowledge by challenging them to identify authors by a selection of opening lines from the authors' most popular novels.

Make It Happen

1. Decide how many weeks to run the contest and choose one *New York Times* bestselling author for each week. The authors chosen should be very popular at your own library and should have a sufficient number of novels that you will always have a least a few in the building.

2. For each author, identify interesting first lines from five of his or her books. To keep the contest from being too challenging, it's best to choose openers from recent titles or older works that are still read regularly. Pick first lines that provide participants with valuable clues, such as character names, place names, or a sense of writing style. Short first lines, like a character's exclamation, are best avoided.

3. Create a sheet for each week that explains the contest rules and lists the five first lines from the week's mystery author. Rules can be basic: a different author will be featured each week, only one entry per participant per week, and answers must be correct in order to be eligible to win. One correct answer from any week should be sufficient to be entered in the final prize drawing; don't expect your patrons to submit answers every week. After the first week, you can note on the bottom of the sheet the identity of the author featured the previous week (Fig. 1.1).

4. Create a poster promoting the program (Fig. 1.2) and answer sheets. You will need to be able to identify which answer sheets correspond with which week in order to know whether responses are correct. Either print each week's answer sheets in a different color or label them by week. The answer sheets should ask the name of the week's mystery author and the patron's name and phone number.

5. Launch the program with a poster, the weekly sheet of first lines, the first-week answer sheets, pencils, an entry box, and the contest prize (Fig. 1.3). Surround these items with books by a variety of different bestselling authors. Use this as an opportunity to promote all of the different material types in your library's collection, by including regular print, large print, books on CD, and any other formats.

6. Consider providing participants with a hint. I noted on the weekly sheet of first lines that the week's mystery author was among those featured in the book display. The challenge of this approach is that you need to follow through and make sure that a book by that author is always on display. Recruit your coworkers to help you in monitoring. Alternative hints could include the first letter of the author's first name or the author's birth year.

Evaluation

Determine participation by counting the number of submitted entries.

Guess the Author: Week 2

Which author wrote these first lines? Complete an entry form with your best guess for a chance to win a Wilton Cast Snowflake Cake Pan. A different author will be featured weekly. One entry allowed per week.

Hint: Books by the featured author are included in this display.

The crisscross-patterned lace curtains, which should have been silk organdy but were rayon instead, billowed in the soft May breeze.

It was dusk when Nikki Quinn stopped her cobalt blue BMW in front of the massive iron gates of Myra Rutledge's McLean estate.

It was a beautiful summer day, but the agitated woman pacing and kneading her hands barely noticed.

Nealy staggered to the corner of Misty Blue's birthing stall, where she leaned against the slatted wall, then slid to the ground.

Davey Taylor didn't like the shine of the street lamp that cut through the darkness and played against the filmy curtains in his bedroom.

Last Week's Author: Stephen King

Figure 1.1 Sheet with five first lines from the week's mystery author (Fern Michaels). Instructions, a hint, and the answer to the previous week's challenge are provided.

From *Librarian's Guide to Passive Programming: Easy and Affordable Activities for All Ages* by Emily T. Wichman. Santa Barbara, CA: Libraries Unlimited. Copyright © 2012.

Guess the Author

See if you can identify NYT bestselling authors by the first lines of their novels during the month of January. Teens and adults may enter once per week. Correct answers will be entered into a grand prize drawing.

January 1-31

during library hours

Adults & Teens

MILFORD-MIAMI TOWNSHIP BRANCH • Clermont County Public Library
1099 State Route 131 • Milford, OH 45150 • 513-248-0700

visit us at www.clermontlibrary.org

Figure 1.2 Guess the Author program poster. Courtesy of Clermont County Public Library and the author.

Figure 1.3 Guess the Author program set up and in progress.

Laid-Back Book Club

Book clubs are a programming staple, with most public libraries offering at least one. While your library is sure to be full of avid readers, I expect only a very small proportion of them attend your book club gatherings. Surely more people are interested in talking about books. What keeps them away? Is it the meeting time? The stress of completing a book by a certain date? The structured nature of the discussion? Fear of sharing ideas in front of a group? Negate these concerns and create some new book club converts with a Laid-Back Book Club!

When Marnie Oakes, now retired, was director of the Reuben Hoar Library (MA), she founded the Laid-Back Book Club after learning about other libraries' attempts to offer informal discussion groups. The Laid-Back Book Club consists of a table with copies of the month's selection, handouts with author information, discussion questions, and a spot to leave comments. All participants have to do is check out the book! While they're encouraged to discuss the book with friends or write down some insights on a return visit, there is absolutely no commitment required. Nine years later, the Book Club is still going strong!

Make It Happen

1. Choose books for the program. There are many websites that provide discussion questions that can serve as a guide. If your library offers other discussion groups, select different titles for the Laid-Back Book Club. Vary selections to appeal to a wider audience; try classics, literary fiction, bestsellers, nonfiction, and so forth. Choose titles that have multiple copies available, preferably in a variety of formats. If getting access to multiple copies of the same book is a challenge, why not offer a series of like books? Patrons could choose from a selection of space operas, books written in the epistolary format, or the mysteries of Agatha Christie. Write questions that examine the intricacies of the genre. Reuben Hoar Library has access through a consortium to book discussion kits, each containing 15 copies of the same title. Similar resources may be available in your area.

2. Decide where the Laid-Back Book Club will be stationed. Reuben Hoar Library has theirs in the lobby (Fig. 1.4), but depending upon the layout of your library, that may put you at risk for losses. Positioning the setup in a high-traffic area is essential. If the display is kept near a service desk, it will be easier to promote and to answer questions. The spot needs to have a table or countertop; a bulletin board hanging above would be ideal.

3. Launch the program by placing copies of the month's book, discussion questions, and author information on the table. Add a publicity poster (Fig. 1.5) and signs making it clear that additional books and other formats can be put on reserve. Establish a method by which participants can share their opinions about the book. When she had access to a bulletin board, Marnie would post the questions there, leaving space for answers to be written. A binder with a page for each question could serve the same purpose.

Evaluation

Make note of how many copies of the selection are put out on the Laid-Back Book Club display throughout the month. At the end of the month, subtract the remaining number of books to find out how many people participated.

Alternative Approaches

With the abundance of easy-to-use Web resources available today, taking the Laid-Back Book Club online is an obvious choice. Create a blog for the Book Club and post each month about the chosen book. Include a link to reserve copies, author information, discussion questions, readalikes, and resources to further explore the book's themes. Participants can leave comments and a moderator can help guide the discussion. Promote the Book Club both online and in the library with posters and copies of the title on display. Evaluate the success of the program by counting the number of comments posted to the blog.

Resources

BookBrowse, "Bookclubs at BookBrowse," http://www.bookbrowse.com/bookclubs/ (cited July 19, 2011).

Reading Group Choices, http://www.readinggroupchoices.com (cited July 19, 2011).

Reading Group Guides, http://www.readinggroupguides.com (cited July 19, 2011).

Figure 1.4 The Laid-Back Book Club, as set up at Reuben Hoar Library. Courtesy of Laura Zalewski.

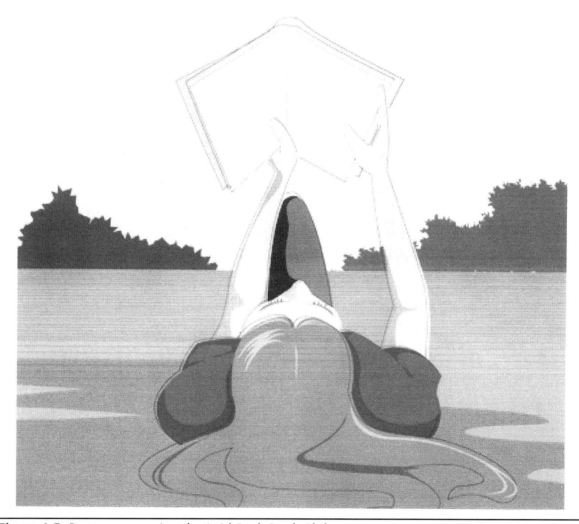

Figure 1.5 Poster promoting the Laid-Back Book Club.

The Literary Gnome

Over the years, I have discovered that some passive programs benefit from a mascot, a character that can draw the patron's eye and be used for promotional purposes. I have made good use of a small gnome statue, creatively dubbed Mr. Gnome, who has instant appeal for children and many adults. When using Mr. Gnome in programs, I'll give away another gnome as a prize. In my experience, this pretty much guarantees good participation numbers. Pick out a character that you think will appeal to your clientele—it doesn't have to be a gnome—and see how incorporating it impacts your programs.

Our patrons are always looking for their next good read, so why not encourage them to share their recommendations with each other? Invite Mr. Gnome to your library to give those readers some incentive! Adults and children alike will happily recommend books for Mr. Gnome to read, especially if doing so gives them a chance to take him home. The recommendations your patrons turn in will give you great material for a book display.

Supplies

- Prize—The prize can be anything, but giving away a gnome (or other character) ties the entire program together.
- Tickets

Make It Happen

1. If you're not a fan of gnomes, pick a different character to feature in your program. Maybe your town or library has a mascot that would be perfect. Having a character isn't essential, but without something eye catching to draw attention to the program, you may find that it's difficult to convince your patrons to take the time to write even brief book reviews.

2. Create forms that have a space for the title and author of the recommended book, along with an area for the participant to write a brief review. Cut down on supply costs by making the forms small enough to fit several on a page (Fig. 1.6).

3. Note in your publicity that the reviews will be posted in the library. Your patrons won't appreciate having their names and contact information on display, so after reviews have been completed, instruct participants to bring them to a staff member. Give the participants tickets on which to record their names and phone numbers, and then draw from these tickets when it comes time to choose a prize winner.

4. Decide if multiple entries will be allowed. I recommend that they are, as the goal of the program is to get patrons sharing books.

5. Launch the program by setting up a display with a program poster (Fig. 1.7), instructions, review forms, pens, and an entry box for the tickets. Be sure to prominently display the prize.

Evaluation

Decide whether you will record the number of individual participants or the number of completed book reviews. Count the tickets accordingly.

Collection Tie-In

While the program is ongoing, begin posting the completed book reviews. Display the books listed, and as you run out of titles, display other books by the same authors.

Alternative Approaches

Promote a different part of your library's collection by changing the name of the program to The Cinematic Gnome (movie reviews), The Musical Gnome (music reviews), or The Electronic Gnome (eMaterial reviews).

The Literary Gnome

Title:

Author:

Mr. Gnome should read this book because:

The Literary Gnome

Title:

Author:

Mr. Gnome should read this book because:

The Literary Gnome

Title:

Author:

Mr. Gnome should read this book because:

The Literary Gnome

Title:

Author:

Mr. Gnome should read this book because:

Figure 1.6 Book recommendation forms, with four fit to a page.

The
Literary Gnome

Mr. Gnome is looking for a good read. Tell him which book you think he should read next and why he might like it. Bring each of your recommendations to the Information Desk for a chance to win your very own gnome. Recommendations will be displayed in the library. Open to all ages.

Figure 1.7 The Literary Gnome program poster.

Mr. Gnome Reads the Classics

After working in the same library for the better part of a decade, I've gotten to know the collection well. I'm sometimes amazed by how many of the books, particularly in fiction, I can identify without even stopping to read the titles. There will be something in the cover design, possibly the font used for the author's name, the positioning of the title, or a familiar graphic that clues me in immediately. This is especially true for some books that have become classics and have maintained the same cover art through multiple printings. There's a certain satisfaction in knowing that you can check out a copy of *The Catcher in the Rye* that looks exactly like the one you read in high school. This program highlights memorable cover art by challenging library visitors to identify classic books from just a portion of the cover image.

Supplies

- Digital camera or scanner

- Gnome—Optional. I've used a small gnome statute to help promote several of my programs. This program can easily be done without a character, but if you choose to use one, it does not have to be a gnome. Consider employing an image of the library's mascot, a favorite pet, a stuffed animal, or something similar.

- Prize—As with other gnome-themed programs, my prize was a gnome statue. Almost any small prize will be incentive for people to participate, as long as you pick something with wide appeal.

Make It Happen

1. Pick four to six books that are well known and have memorable cover art. To keep the program accessible for both children and adults, all of my selections were children's titles. The books I chose to feature were: *Green Eggs and Ham* by Dr. Seuss, *A Wrinkle in Time* by Madeleine L'Engle, *Goodnight Moon* by Margaret Wise Brown, *Charlotte's Web* by E. B. White, *Little House on the Prairie* by Laura Ingalls Wilder, and *The Giving Tree* by Shel Silverstein.

2. When selecting titles, set aside whichever copy's cover is in the best condition. Use a digital camera or scanner to capture images of the book covers. Open the images in a graphics editing program and crop each one so that only a portion of the cover art is visible. If you have chosen to use a gnome or other character to promote the program, consider inserting a small picture of the character into the cropped cover art image.

3. Print large color copies of each cropped image and use them to create a poster display for the program. Number each of the photographs. Incorporate an explanation of the challenge. My poster included the program name and the following text: "There's a gnome loose in the library! Can you guess what he's been reading? He'll come home with one lucky person who can correctly identify all of the books he's reading."

4. Create an answer sheet with small black-and-white images of each cropped cover. Number the pictures in the same manner used on the poster. Require participants to identify each book by author and title. Make sure to ask for patron names and phone numbers so that the winner can be notified (Fig. 1.8).

5. Launch the program by setting up your poster in a prominent area. Put out the answer sheets, something to write with, and an entry box for completed sheets. Display the prize with a "Win Me" sign to draw attention (Fig. 1.9).

Evaluation

Count the number of completed answer sheets to determine the number of participants.

Alternative Approaches

This program could easily be run in the library's newsletter or on the library's website. Feature all of the covers at once, or spread them out over a period of time. Create an online form for participants to submit their answers.

Instead of books, use movie or album covers for your cropped images. Popular movies, in particular, are recognizable to both children and adults.

Mr. Gnome Reads the Classics

There's a gnome loose in the library! Can you tell what he's been reading?

| #1 | #2 | #3 | #4 | #5 | #6 |

Book #1

    Title: _____

    Author: _____

Book #2

    Title: _____

    Author: _____

Book #3

    Title: _____

    Author: _____

Book #4

    Title: _____

    Author: _____

Book #5

    Title: _____

    Author: _____

Book #6

    Title: _____

    Author: _____

Name: _____ Phone Number: _____

Figure 1.8 Mr. Gnome Reads the Classics answer sheet.

Figure 1.9 Mr. Gnome Reads the Classics program set up and in progress.

Name That Story

The Children's Department staff at Marion Public Library (OH) has found that they have great success with self-directed programming during summer reading. In 2010, library staffer Marguarite Markley took a series of photographs of a stuffed animal surrounded by props, arranged to depict familiar children's book titles. Kids were challenged to guess which book was represented by each image. The contest was promoted in the summer reading packets each child received, and a new photograph was released each week on the library's website. While the library's summer reading program provided a built-in audience for this contest, Name That Story is an activity that can be offered at any time during the year. Barbara Moore, Children's and Branch Services Head for Marion Public Library, provided tips on how to make this program a reality.

Supplies

- Stuffed animal or doll—Pick a fun character that is large enough to be posed with props and dressed in clothing.
- Props—Items required will depend upon book titles chosen.
- Digital camera—A tripod may prove helpful.
- Prize—Marion Public Library awarded its winner a gift basket full of paperback books and small toys.

Make It Happen

1. Begin by deciding which ages will be invited to participate in the contest. Marion Public Library's program was for children 12 and under, which is reflected in the titles the staff chose to depict in photographs. If including teens and adults, consider creating a separate set of images featuring age-appropriate books.

2. Picking book titles for the photographs takes some thought. The books should be sufficiently popular as to be well known among the library's users. Multiple-word titles containing terms that can be easily depicted with props are essential. The books that Marion Public Library selected are given in the following section.

3. Take some time to plan each photograph. What supplies are needed? Where is the best place to take the picture? Have ideas and props for one or two photographs beyond the number needed for the program. If unexpected problems arise while taking pictures in the field, it will be easier to switch gears with supplies on hand than to go back to the library and have to scramble for alternatives.

4. Wait for a nice day to hold the photo shoot. Marion Public Library staff took several of their photographs at local businesses, such as a car dealer and a movie theater. Barbara reports that while employees at these establishments will likely be amused by your request to photograph a stuffed animal on the premises, they are unlikely to turn you down. Depending upon your library's policies, a signed permission form may be required for these photographs, particularly if they include identifiable individuals.

5. Determine whether the program will be held online, physically in the library, or both. Post the pictures and create an entry form that, for each image, includes a space for every letter in the title and the author's name. This extra clue will help participants identify the correct books.

6. When the program is over, award a prize to one randomly drawn participant. Marion Public Library required those eligible for the prize to have correctly identified all 10 books. Of 110 entries, approximately 60 were successful.

Sample Book and Staging Suggestions

Eating the Alphabet by Lois Ehlert: stuffed animal with a bowl of letters, sitting at a picnic table (Fig. 1.10)

If You Take a Mouse to the Movies by Laura Numeroff: stuffed animal dressed as a mouse or accompanied by a mouse, posed at a movie theater concession stand

Harold and the Purple Crayon by Crockett Johnson: stuffed animal holding a purple crayon, purple masking tape applied to a wall to look like crayon marks (Fig. 1.11)

The Lightning Thief by Rick Riordan: stuffed animal held by a police officer, wearing a mask, holding a thunderbolt

The Mouse and the Motorcycle by Beverly Cleary: stuffed animal dressed as a mouse, sitting on a motorcycle (Fig. 1.12)

The Rainbow Fish by Marcus Pfister: stuffed animal in front of a fish tank, holding a rainbow

Captain Underpants by Dav Pilkey: stuffed animal dressed as a pirate, wearing men's briefs (Fig. 1.13)

The Boxcar Children by Gertrude Chandler Warner: stuffed animal in a box, stuffed animal sitting in a car, stuffed animal with a group of children, images strung together with plus signs

Evaluation

The number of contest entries will equal the number of participants.

Alternative Approaches

Prior to 2010, Marion Public Library offered a modified version of this program during summer reading. A character was chosen depending upon the year's theme, one time a praying mantis, another time a Hawaiian dancer. The character was photographed at sites around the community and contest participants had to identify the locations.

Figure 1.10 A stuffed animal seated at a picnic table, eating a bowl full of letters, suggests Lois Ehlert's book, *Eating the Alphabet*. Courtesy of Marguarite Markley.

Figure 1.11 A purple crayon and accompanying marks on the wall could only represent *Harold and the Purple Crayon* by Crockett Johnson. Courtesy of Marguarite Markley.

Figure 1.12 Paper ears and pipe cleaner whiskers turn this stuffed animal into a mouse for Beverly Cleary's *The Mouse and the Motorcycle*. Courtesy of Marguarite Markley.

Figure 1.13 Any *Captain Underpants* fan is sure to get a kick out of a stuffed animal dressed in an eye patch and baggy undies! Courtesy of Marguarite Markley.

Our Books Go Far

When I'm in the stacks, shelving or weeding, I sometimes wonder about the journey each book has taken since it was originally purchased for the library. Sand, food stains, greasy fingerprints, and annotated pages all provide clues. We know our materials venture far outside our service areas, because occasionally forgotten items will be shipped back home. Just recently, a box from a rental agency in Hilton Head arrived at my southwestern Ohio library containing an escaped book. This next summer, encourage your patrons to make reading a part of their vacations, and at the same time, learn a little bit about where your materials have traveled. Invite users to send the library a postcard stating what book they've read or to take a picture of themselves reading on vacation. This is a fun activity for any age and the submissions make a great display.

Supplies

- United States map

- World map

- Straight pins—Get the kind with the big, colorful heads.

- Foam board

- Old maps and travel brochures

- Tickets

- Prize—Pick a travel-themed prize within your budget. You may want to consider one prize for adults and one for kids. Possible prizes include: travel clocks, toiletry bags, emergency weather radios, road atlases, emergency car kits, water bottles, backpacks, travel guides, etc.

Make It Happen

1. Decide on the easiest way to run this program at your library. Choose one or both of the following methods. Either have patrons bring or mail a postcard to the library listing which book was read while on vacation, or have patrons bring in a vacation photo showing themselves reading at their destination. If you opt to have patrons submit photos, be prepared to be asked if the photographs can be submitted online. Determine how you will answer this question.

2. Since each photo or postcard submitted will be an entry to win the prize, be sure to decide whether multiple entries are allowed. I recommend permitting one entry per family member per destination.

3. Plan to run the program all summer long, June through August. Start promotion in May so that people taking vacations early in the summer have time to prepare.

4. Create an instruction sheet for your patrons to take along on vacation (Fig. 1.14). If they are to mail in postcards or e-mail photos, be sure to include the proper addresses. Note on the instructions that pictures and postcards will be displayed in the library.

5. Mount the United States map and the world map on foam board. As entries are received, mark the maps with straight pins, so that everyone can see all the destinations the library's books have traveled to. If you're uncomfortable using pins, the locations can be marked with dot stickers.

6. Choose a way to display the postcards and photographs that are received. If you have a bulletin board, wall, or shelving end panel by your display area, those are obvious choices. If not, attach the items to a large piece of foam board propped up with an easel.

7. Launch the program by decorating the area with old maps and travel brochures. The maps, in particular, make a great backdrop for displaying the submissions. Set up your U.S. and world maps. Display the prize with a "Win Me!" sign. Have lots of instruction sheets available and an entry box. For each photo or postcard turned in, have participants fill out a prize drawing ticket with their name and phone number.

Evaluation

Determine the number of participants by counting the number of prize drawing tickets or the number of postcards and pictures submitted. Decide whether you want to count individual entries or individual participants.

Collection Tie-In

- Travel guides and films
- Travel memoirs
- State and country books
- Beach reads
- Audio books appropriate for the whole family

Alternative Approaches

If you choose to have your patrons only submit photographs, this is the perfect program to run through the library's website. Provide submission instructions and have participants acknowledge that their pictures will be posted on the library's website. Gather names and contact information so that prize winners can be notified.

Our Books Go Far

Did you take your library books on vacation?

Let us know where you went and what you read!

Each participant will be entered in a drawing to win an American Red Cross AM/FM/NOAA Solar/Crank Power Portable Radio.

Here's what you need to do:

Bring us a postcard from your vacation spot, listing which book you read while on your trip.

-OR-

Bring us a vacation photo that shows you holding your library book.

Stop at the Information Desk with your postcard or photo to enter the drawing.

The Fine Print: Postcards and photos will be displayed in the library. Multiple postcards and photos from different locations or different family members can be used to enter the drawing multiple times.

June-August

Milford-Miami Township Branch Library

Figure 1.14 Instruction sheet for Our Books Go Far program.

From *Librarian's Guide to Passive Programming: Easy and Affordable Activities for All Ages* by Emily T. Wichman. Santa Barbara, CA: Libraries Unlimited. Copyright © 2012.

Shredded Book Contest

One surefire way to draw attention to something is to ban it, destroy it, or repurpose it. On the dark side of the literary world, that can mean material challenges and book burnings, but there is a brighter outlook also. The altered book as an art form is growing in popularity, while typing "crafts with old books" into an Internet search engine will produce dozens of recycling possibilities. No doubt your library discards numerous damaged books each year and also receives donated books in poor condition. Give some of these books new life by hosting a Shredded Book Contest, an activity sure to spark immediate interest in young library visitors.

For several years during the annual summer reading program, Lynn Montague of Sun Prairie Public Library (WI) has shredded a popular children's book, put it in a jar, and challenged patrons to identify the book. Each week brings a new shredded book and up to 200 kids guessing its title. Betsy Bromley of Oconomowoc Public Library (WI) learned of this contest from Lynn and has had great success presenting a similar program to her patrons. Betsy reports that, "It's really fun to watch the kids see the book for the first time, realize what it is, and then get really excited to figure it out." Betsy also likes the program because children often need to use the catalog in order to identify the books, which improves their search skills.

Supplies

- Books—Monitor discards and donations for popular children's books. Series books such as *Harry Potter, Captain Underpants, Magic School Bus*, and *Junie B. Jones* are good choices. Both picture books and chapter books are suitable. Paperbacks are easiest to work with.

- Shredder—It is important to have a shredder that cuts paper coarse enough that occasional words can be read. A confetti-style shredder would not be a suitable choice.

- Jar—Obtain a clear jar large enough to hold a shredded book. Betsy has had good luck with a 12-cup canister. Either clean up an old food container or shop at a home goods store for something new.

- Clear packing tape

- Resealable bags—1-gallon size

- Prizes—Both Sun Prairie and Oconomowoc Public Libraries give away books. If your library receives donated books, this is a good source for prizes.

Make It Happen

1. Decide how long the contest will run and obtain one book appropriate for shredding for each week. Write the names of the books on resealable bags.

2. Shred each book one at a time. Take care to monitor the results of the shredding. You want pieces big enough to allow for some readable words, but you don't want so many keywords visible that the book title can be guessed at a mere glance. Rotate the direction pages are fed into the shredder so that some are shredded vertically, others horizontally. Once all of the pages have been removed, the shredder should be able to handle the covers and binding of a paperback. Run these through to add color and additional clues. If shredding a hardcover book, also shred the book jacket. Once a book has been shredded, put it into the appropriate bag.

3. Place the first shredded book to be featured in the contest in the clear jar. Expect the jar to be handled heavily by children examining its contents. Discourage little hands from opening the jar by reinforcing the seal with clear packing tape.

4. At Sun Prairie Public Library, Lynn chooses to write a clue that corresponds to each shredded book. You might consider taking this approach if you find after the first week or two that participants are having difficulty guessing the titles, or if you've picked some less familiar books to shred. Example clues that Lynn has used in the past are given in the following section.

5. Create a sign for the program that explains what the contest is and how to participate (Fig. 1.15). Create entry forms that ask for name, contact information, and the title and author of the shredded book.

6. If your library makes outreach visits to schools, bring a jar containing a shredded book along, and tell students about the program. Betsy finds that children are always eager to examine the jar!

7. When it's time to launch the program, create a display that includes the shredded book jar, the sign explaining the contest and its rules, entry forms, an entry box, and pencils. If your contest will feature multiple shredded books, consider including a sign that states the last day to guess the current book, the day the answer will be revealed, and the day the next book will be displayed (Fig. 1.16).

8. Each week, pick a winner from those children who correctly identified the book. Place the shredded book back in its plastic bag and present it to the child. If possible, gather a selection of donated children's books and let each winner pick one intact book for an additional prize.

9. When setting out the next shredded book, provide notice of the title of the previous week's book, how many entries were received, and how many people guessed correctly (Fig. 1.17).

Sample Clues Describing Shredded Books

Viking Ships at Sunrise by Mary Pope Osborne: Jack and Annie make a splash in this adventure.

Because of Winn-Dixie by Kate DiCamillo: This dog story won an award.

Ramona the Pest by Beverly Cleary: The main character starts kindergarten.

Frog and Toad Together by Arnold Lobel: Amphibian friends have adventures together.

Madeline's Rescue by Ludwig Bemelmans: This rhyming tale is set in Europe.

Froggy Plays in the Band by Jonathan London: One mustn't stop for anything in this book!

Stellaluna by Janell Cannon: Pip and Flap are two characters in this story.

Evaluation

Count the number of entries submitted each week. Since entry forms include names, you can track both the number of unique contestants and the frequency with which they participated.

Alternative Approaches

Participation in the Shredded Book Contest is limited to children at the Sun Prairie and Oconomowoc Public Libraries, but both Lynn and Betsy have seen parents as interested in the contest as their children. Why not try creating a version geared especially for adults? Keep an eye out for books that are likely to be familiar to a wide audience. Classics would be a good choice, as would books that have been made into movies.

Shredded Book Contest!

How to Play:
- There is a **shredded book** in this jar. Every part of the book is included, even the cover and spine.
- Pick up the jar, shake it around, and examine it closely to try and figure out what book it is. Picture books **and** chapter books are possible answers.
- The jar must remain closed at all times.
- Enter your guess in the jar. At the end of the week, Betsy will draw a winner from all correct guesses. The winner will be contacted about his or her prize.
- Don't worry, the shredded book was ruined or no longer usable! Don't try this at home!
- We will have more shredded books out this summer, so if at first you don't succeed, try, try again!

Figure 1.15 Sign explaining the guidelines for participating in the contest. Courtesy of Betsy Bromley.

Last day to guess this Shredded Book:

Answer revealed:

New Shredded Book contest starting:

Figure 1.16 Sign indicating important contest dates. Sign should be updated each time a new shredded book is displayed. Courtesy of Lynn Montague.

From *Librarian's Guide to Passive Programming: Easy and Affordable Activities for All Ages* by Emily T. Wichman. Santa Barbara, CA: Libraries Unlimited. Copyright © 2012.

Answer for Shredded Book June 9 - June 22:

Frog and Toad Together

154 kids took a guess.

33 kids guessed correctly and won a free book!

Figure 1.17 Sign revealing the title of the previous week's shredded book and participation details. The Sun Prairie Public Library awards a prize to each child that correctly identifies the book. Courtesy of Lynn Montague.

Chapter 2

Writing

In order to appreciate the work that goes into crafting an entertaining story or writing a clear and engaging piece of nonfiction, it's good to do a bit of your own writing from time to time. Many people have daydreams about writing the next great American novel, and lots of folks enjoy writing just for fun. Maybe your library even hosts a writers' group. The programs in this chapter will have your patrons creating and sharing stories, some original and some of personal experience. In One Story, Many Authors, participants each contribute a couple of sentences to a story that has the potential to lead anywhere. Library visitors can try their hand at comedy with Crazy Captions. Almost everyone is intrigued by celebrities, so Celebrity Encounters gives patrons an opportunity to reminisce about times they've had a brush with fame. Provide teens an opportunity to share their thoughts and improve their writing skills by establishing a Writing Center. There are plenty of ways to get your patrons writing, be it short story contests, reminiscing exercises, or review writing. With a little imagination, you'll think of all sorts of options!

Celebrity Encounters

Pulling off a last-minute program that relates to current events in your community can be difficult, especially if you have to contract with a performer or work with another department to meet publicity deadlines. As programmers, we take our best guess based on what we know of our community's interests and needs, and then keep our fingers crossed for good attendance. That being the case, it's especially satisfying when a program planned several months in advance turns out to complement an issue or event that has suddenly become popular.

This happened to me in 2011. I planned a passive program in which patrons were asked share stories and photographs from their encounters with celebrities, thinking it would tie-in with February's Oscar buzz. When planning the program, I was not aware that it would coincide with the arrival in town of George Clooney, who was filming scenes for an upcoming picture. Movie news and Clooney sightings became a hot topic in the region's media, and as an unexpected result, my little program was featured on a local news channel's website. While, alas, none of my participants reported on a Clooney encounter, I did receive stories about a variety of famous people, from Johnny Bench to Johnny Cash.

Make It Happen

1. Begin by deciding how participants will submit their celebrity stories and photographs, either in person or online. Because my program was held at only one location in a multibranch system, I had people submit entries in print format at my library.

2. Create a story submission form (Fig. 2.1). At the top of the page, explain the program and provide the run dates. Since photographs will be posted, check your library's guidelines to see if you need to add wording about participants granting permission for their stories and photos to be displayed. Leave a sizable space for people to record the name of the celebrity they met and to relate the accompanying story. At the bottom of the page, make a cutoff entry form that asks for the participant's name and contact information. Consider having participants drop off the forms at the service desk so you can be sure of displaying the proper stories and photographs together.

3. The program will draw more attention if you have some stories and photographs already on hand for the first day. Ask coworkers, friends, and family members, and you're sure to find out about a few celebrity sightings.

4. Create an area to display the stories and images. A bulletin board or empty wall located near a table works well. If you only have a countertop or table, you can create a display area with a large decorated piece of poster board propped up on an easel. Decorate with celebrity-themed graphics like stars, red carpet, cameras, limos, and autographs. Celebrities don't just have to be movie stars. Posting words such as musician, politician, athlete, author, comedian, and chef will encourage people to think more broadly about encounters they can write about.

5. A prize is always a good incentive for these types of programs. I gave away a puzzle book featuring celebrities. For those with limited funds, a selection of good-condition, donated DVDs can make a nice gift. If you're able to splurge, how about a "Treat Yourself Like a Celebrity" gift basket filled with a few small luxury items?

6. Launch the program with the display, a publicity poster (Fig. 2.2), story submission forms, pens, and an entry box. Be sure to show off the prize!

Evaluation

Count the number of entries submitted to determine participation. Since the goal is to gather tales of a wide variety of celebrities, encourage participants to enter as many times as they have stories.

Collection Tie-In

- Biographies
- Memoirs
- Novels written by celebrities
- Children's books written by celebrities

Alternative Approaches

This would be an excellent program to take online. Imagine the conversation that could get started in the comments of a blog post requesting celebrity stories! If posting people's pictures online, you'll definitely want to establish a procedure for granting permission.

Dream up supplemental celebrity-themed activities. How about a quiz requiring people to match the baby name to the celebrity couple? Or a challenge to identify celebrities by their quotes? If a major awards event like the Oscars is on the horizon, post the nominees and let people vote on who they think will win.

Celebrity Encounters
February 1-28

If you've ever met someone famous, we'd like to hear your story and see the evidence! One person will win a prize. Here's what you need to do:

Complete the "My Story" and "Entry Form" sections below. If possible, bring in a photograph of yourself with the famous person you met. Turn in this paper and your photo at the Information Desk. By submitting your story and photo, you grant permission for them to be displayed in the library for the length of the program

My Story

I met:

Here's how it happened:

Entry Form

Name: _____

Phone Number: _____

Celebrity Encounters
February 1-28

If you've ever met someone famous, we'd like to hear your story and see the evidence! One person will win a prize. Here's what you need to do:

Complete the "My Story" and "Entry Form" sections below. If possible, bring in a photograph of yourself with the famous person you met. Turn in this paper and your photo at the Information Desk. By submitting your story and photo, you grant permission for them to be displayed in the library for the length of the program

My Story

I met:

Here's how it happened:

Entry Form

Name: _____

Phone Number: _____

Figure 2.1 Combined story submission form and prize drawing entry form, designed to fit two per page.

Celebrity Encounters

Submit photos or stories of times you have met famous people and receive an entry to win a copy of **Brain Games: Celebrity Puzzles**. Receive one entry for each photo or story you submit. Photos and stories will be displayed in the library.

February 1–28

Adults & Teens

MILFORD-MIAMI TOWNSHIP BRANCH • Clermont County Public Library
1099 State Route 131 • Milford, OH 45150 • 513-248-0700

visit us at www.clermontlibrary.org

Figure 2.2 Poster advertising the Celebrity Encounters program. Courtesy of Clermont County Public Library and the author.

Crazy Captions

Have you ever looked at a photo, particularly of an animal, and wondered what it was thinking? Probably every pet owner has at one time captured some of their pet's crazy antics on film. Invite library patrons to get creative and speculate on what those animals might have to say if they could talk. Post some pictures, leave room for people to write captions, and you're bound to get plenty of funny responses. Not only will adults have fun contributing, but you'll be pleased to see kids working with each other and their parents to dream up one-liners. When I hosted this program at my library, it was called "Crazy Cat Captions" and featured goofy images of my coworker's cats.

Supplies

- Photographs—Select images that lend themselves to writing captions.
- Easel
- Easel paper

Make It Happen

1. Select two to four photographs that will inspire your audience to write creative and funny captions (Fig. 2.3–Fig. 2.5). Pet pictures work well and should be easy to obtain from coworkers if you don't have your own. Wildlife photos or images of anthropomorphic statuary can work well also. You or your coworkers probably have a wealth of funny pictures of your children. If you have the parents' permission, and can do so without mortifying the child in question, consider using kid pictures. The appeal of a cute child is universal!

2. Decide how to display the photographs you have selected, remembering that plenty of room is needed to write captions beside the corresponding images. I had good success using an easel, because it can be set up anywhere and is at the appropriate height for most people to write. Attach a large pad of paper to the easel and put the title of the program across the top, followed by simple instructions: "What were these animals/kids thinking?!? Share your theory by writing captions below each picture." Attach the pictures to the paper, leaving writing space near each one.

3. Launch the program by setting up the easel in a high-traffic area. Be sure to have pens or pencils on hand. Attaching the pen to the easel with a long piece of string will cut down on the number of lost writing implements. If the comments area gets full, cut a piece of paper to size and attach it to the space, creating a flap. More comments can be added and the old ones can be read by lifting the paper.

4. Any public writing project of this sort needs some monitoring. Decide in advance how you are going to handle captions that aren't in the spirit of a family program. If you plan to remove comments that you deem inappropriate for your community, you may want to include a disclaimer on your display. When selecting the pictures, save yourself a lot of grief by taking a moment to examine the image and consider its potential for risqué humor.

Evaluation

Count the number of captions written to determine the number of participants.

Collection Tie-In

- Photography books

- Pet or animal books tied to the images on display

- Joke books

- Humorous works of fiction or nonfiction

Alternative Approaches

Use this program as an opportunity to partner with your local high school drama class or theater group. Ask members of either to use their props and costumes to stage a series of images appropriate for captioning. Make sure to get the proper permissions so that you can use the resulting photographs for your program.

Stretch this idea into both a passive program and a traditional program. Host an event for children or teens, specifically for the purpose of creating images for the Crazy Captions program. Give the attendees costumes and props and see what they can come up with. Again, be sure to get permissions.

Take this program online, posting the photos on the library's website. Create a form that allows users to submit their captions.

Figure 2.3 This inquisitive titmouse surely has something to say!

Figure 2.4 What's on this deer's mind?

Figure 2.5 This Biltmore Estate grotesque appears to be deep in thought.

One Story, Many Authors

A significant portion of any public library's patrons are users primarily because they are story junkies. These people love to be drawn into the plot of a book or movie. Quite a few of them probably have secret dreams of writing their own books. Tap into this ardor by giving library visitors an easy opportunity to craft a story. Hang up a large piece of paper, write an intriguing opening line, and invite people to each add a sentence to the tale.

Make It Happen

1. Every story needs an engaging start, so choose the first sentence for this group writing project carefully. Do you want a first line that's vague enough to launch stories in multiple genres, or do you want to use a line that will play off other programs offered by the library? The opener could be something of your own creation, the classic "It was a dark and stormy night...," or maybe the first line from a recent book club selection or community reading program title. A few examples from my own hand are given in the following section.

2. A large writing surface is required for this project. A good possibility is an easel with a pad of blank paper. Other options include white boards, paper-covered bulletin boards, or simply a large sheet of paper taped to the wall. The story should be positioned in a prominent location, such as by a service desk, so that it can be easily promoted and monitored. Additionally, promote the program through normal channels, such as with a program poster (Fig. 2.6), event calendar entry, and press releases.

3. Set up the activity by writing the chosen first line across the top of the page. So that there's always something handy to write with, tie a pen or pencil to a long piece of string and secure it nearby.

4. The story needs to be monitored as it grows to make sure that the content stays family-friendly. Decide in advance how you will handle this problem if it arises. Will you erase inappropriate statements, or start the story over fresh? Changing the location of the story within the building might help. I recommend a prominent sign at the top of the story, maybe a starburst printed in a neon color, requesting that all story contributions be kept at a PG level.

5. When it's time to end the program, post the story in the library for a few weeks so that everyone can have a chance to read it. You may want to transcribe the text for clarity. Don't leave readers with a cliffhanger! Staff can write the final sentences to wrap up the story, or invite a book club, writing group, or teen advisory board to take care of that for you.

Sample Opening Lines

A voice was screaming in the night, "Help! Somebody please help me!"

A figure lurched through the blizzard conditions, wrapped so tightly in layers of winter gear that a passerby would not have known if the person as male or female, young or old.

"This might just be the worst day ever," mused Caleb, as the bell rang and the previously silent hallway suddenly filled with students.

Alice stood on the deck of the massive ocean liner, waiving furiously to the friends and family that had come to see her off.

The spacecraft decelerated as it approached Earth and prepared to enter a low orbit.

I awoke in the middle of the night to a loud commotion that sounded like it was coming from the barn.

"Think of today as the first day of the rest of your life," said my soon-to-be former boss, without even a hint of irony, as he handed me my pink slip.

James stepped into his time machine and thought, "When should I go today?"

Evaluation

Count the number of different sentences added to the story to determine participation. Handwriting changes should make the transitions between authors obvious.

Collection Tie-In

- Interactive books where the reader directs the ending

- Novels featuring memorable first lines

- Writing guides

Alternative Approach

Modify the idea for this program just a bit, and turn it into a short story writing contest. Pick a first line that's vague enough that it could start off stories in a variety of genres. Set a word limit and invite participants to craft a story featuring the chosen opening line. This is a great opportunity to partner with junior high and high school English teachers and to encourage the involvement of writing groups. Consider asking local authors to submit their own stories in advance of the program, and allow them to be used for promotional purposes. Publish entries on the library's website and, if funds allow, assemble a booklet of the best stories for distribution. Readers should enjoy perusing the variety of tales that spring from a single shared sentence.

One Story, Many Authors

If a story started....

Alice stood on the deck of the massive ocean liner, waiving furiously to the friends and family that had come to see her off.

What do you think would happen next? Where is Alice going? Why is she leaving home? What adventures await her?

Participate in a cooperative writing project and help tell Alice's story.

April – During library hours

Figure 2.6 One Story, Many Authors program poster.

Writing Center

Cindy Rider wanted to find a way to promote the connection between reading and writing skills while providing an ongoing enrichment activity for visitors to Vigo County Public Library's (IN) Young People's Department. With the inspiration that sometimes comes from a sleepless night, Cindy created the Writing Center, a special area set aside in the library for the purpose of encouraging older children and teens to express themselves through writing. At a special table, youth are supplied with notebooks and tools to inspire their creativity. Though a relatively new program, the Writing Center is off to a successful start with Vigo County kids logging daily entries in the notebooks.

Supplies

- Composition book
- Pencil
- Hook-and-loop fastening tape
- Sheet protectors
- Rhyming dictionary
- Youth thesaurus

Make It Happen

1. Determine the target audience for the Writing Center and let that guide you in deciding where to locate it. You'll need a table that can be taken over long term with supplies for the program. A location that is near comfortable seating is ideal. A Writing Center is an obvious choice for a library's teen area, but consider any space in the building where people linger. If you find this program to be successful with your young adult users, then give adult patrons an opportunity to write also!

2. Create a sign explaining what the Writing Center is and how to participate (Fig. 2.7). Invite visitors to write a story or a poem. Encourage them to keep their writing "school appropriate." Recommend that if children sign their work, they do so only with their first name and age.

3. Gather together a selection of tools to help participants develop topics to write about. Cindy compiled lists of writing prompts and bound them together in sheet protectors. See the Resources section for assistance in finding prompts. Consider adding some helpful books from the library's collection, such as a rhyming dictionary and thesaurus.

4. Launch the Writing Center by putting out one or two notebooks, the writing prompts, books, and sign. Cindy used hook-and-loop fastening tape to attach a pencil to the cover of each notebook (Fig. 2.8).

5. Focus on word-of-mouth promotion to develop an audience for this program. Do you know which of your regulars like to write? Invite them to make the initial contributions to the notebooks. Keep an eye out for kids who seem bored or have been in the building for hours. They're a prime audience for any new activity.

6. Think ahead about what to do with filled notebooks. You'll most certainly want to keep them in the general vicinity of the Writing Center so that others can continue to enjoy reading them. The library could even catalog the notebooks as reference items. This would be a wonderful way to acknowledge the value of participants' contributions.

Evaluation

Check the notebooks each day and write the date next to each new entry. This process will make it easy to track the number of contributions. If completed notebooks are cataloged, usage statistics will further reveal the impact of the program, by giving a sense of how many people are reading the stories and poems.

Collection Tie-In

- Additional prompt books—What other materials might inspire a person's writing? Rotate through art books, quote books, visual dictionaries, timelines, and anything else intriguing.

- Writer's guides

- Author memoirs and biographies

Alternative Approaches

Cindy Simerlink of Dayton Metro Library (OH) has created a group response program she calls What's Yours? that gets the teens at her library sharing their thoughts. On an end panel in the teen area, Cindy hangs a large, blank piece of paper (Fig. 2.9). Each month a different question is written across the top of the sheet, along with an invitation to "Share your thoughts!" and a warning to "Keep it clean!" To kick off each new question, ask a teen to write the first response. Make markers available and additional comments will follow. Some of Cindy's past questions have included:

- What present do you most want to receive this December?

- What's your New Year's resolution?

- Name the celebrity most likely to spend Valentine's Day alone.

- What author's books do you read as soon as they come out?

- What's the best book you read this year?

- What's your favorite book from your childhood?

Resources

CanTeach, "Writing Prompts/Journal Topics," http://www.canteach.ca/elementary/prompts.html (cited July 19, 2011).

Gallipoli, Linda, "#1492. Journal Writing Ideas," Teachers.Net, http://teachers.net/lessons/posts/1492.html (cited July 19, 2011).

Lewis, Beth, "Journal Prompts for Young Creative Writers," http://k6educators.about.com/od/languageart1/qt/jpromptsx.htm (cited July 19, 2011).

Schoenberg, Jill, "Journal Buddies," http://journalbuddies.com (cited July 19, 2011).

WRITING CENTER

Open a notebook and write a
story, poem, etc. and illustrate it
if you wish. Please keep the
content "school-appropriate."
You may sign it with your FIRST
name and GRADE in school.
If you need help getting started,
you may select a prompt
from the list.

Brought to you by

YOUNG PEOPLE'S
DEPARTMENT

and PALS
(Partners Advancing
Literacy Skills)

Figure 2.7 Sign explaining how to participate in the Writing Center. Courtesy of Cindy Rider.

Figure 2.8 The Writing Center, as set up at Vigo County Public Library. Courtesy of Cindy Rider.

Figure 2.9 One of the posters from Cindy Simerlink's What's Yours? program full of responses from Dayton Metro Library teens. Courtesy of Cindy Simerlink.

Chapter 3

Mysteries

The programs in this chapter are all about analyzing clues to solve a mystery. In the Mystery Theme Contest, patrons study the covers of books on display to determine the common theme. Whodunit? is perfect for theatrical staff members who get photographed in costume. After reading the description of a crime, participants study a photo lineup of potential criminals and discover the perpetrator based on a series of clues. Mystery readers will get a kick out of trying to solve "minute mysteries" in Get a Clue. While these mystery programs don't require a lot of supplies, the planning process is probably the most labor intensive of any passive program type featured in this book. A mystery isn't a mystery if it isn't tricky, so be sure to allow enough time to design a cunning program. The mystery genre is extremely popular, so you should have no trouble finding an audience for these activities. The same people who enjoy mystery programs may also like the scavenger hunts described in the following chapter.

Get a Clue

Sometime in your childhood, you probably heard the riddle about the man who hung himself in a room, completely empty, except for a puddle of water. "How did he hang himself with nothing to climb on?" you were asked. If you have a knack for logic puzzles, you might have correctly answered that the man climbed on a block of ice, which later melted. Did you grow up to love mysteries? Many of our library users did! Clermont County Public Library (OH) tapped into the popularity of this genre by creating a mini mystery contest. Each week, library visitors had the opportunity to read a brief mystery and take a stab at solving it correctly for the chance to win a prize. Kelly Clark was a member of the committee that designed this program and provided tips on how to pull it off, along with one of the stories she wrote.

Make It Happen

1. Before getting started with this program, you need to find people to write four short mysteries. If you don't feel up to this yourself, ask around and find out which of your coworkers enjoy writing. You should be tripping over them, working in a library! Alternatively, you could ask local authors or members of a creative writing group to supply stories.

2. Provide authors with some basic guidelines to ensure that their stories meet the needs of the program. Each mystery will have to fit on a handout, so set a maximum length somewhere around 400 words. Require a question at the end of each story asking about the solution to the mystery. Determine the audience for the program to make sure authors are writing at an appropriate reading level. Clermont County Public Library's contest was open to patrons 18 years of age and older.

3. For story-writing inspiration, visit some of the websites in the Resources section below. Many more short mysteries are available online and can be found using search terms such as "mini mysteries," "two-minute mysteries," and "five-minute mysteries." In the following section, read a story Kelly wrote for one week of Clermont County Public Library's contest. To solve her mystery, it was necessary for readers to be familiar with the library system's hours of operation. You might choose to add a hint at the end of each mystery. Doing so will increase the number of patrons who correctly solve the mystery and will make the game accessible to a wider range of ages.

4. Each week of the program will feature a new mystery, so it is necessary to create four different handouts. Begin each handout with a list of instructions for participating in the contest. People will need to read the story, answer the question that follows, provide contact information, and drop the completed sheet off in the entry box. Note any age restrictions and that only one entry may be submitted per week. Following the instructions, include the full text of the week's story on the handout. A question about the mystery's solution should immediately follow, along with any hint. Leave sufficient space for participants to write in their answers and provide blanks for name and phone number.

5. Launch the program by putting out the appropriate handouts for the first week. In addition, you'll need a program poster (Fig. 3.1), pens, an entry box, and information about the prize being offered. At the start of each new week, swap out the handouts for a new mystery. Patrons will want to know whether they solved each mystery correctly, so be sure to reveal whodunit (or how they did it) the following week.

Sample Mystery: *Pookie's Inheritance* by Kelly Clark

Old Mrs. Henderson was found dead in her bedroom last Sunday morning. Forensics determined her death occurred sometime between 6:00 and 7:00 p.m. Saturday night. A gun left at the scene suggested foul play and Detective Summers was on the case.

Detective Summers spent the day questioning people in Mrs. Henderson's neighborhood. One of her neighbors had seen Mrs. Henderson's son going into the house around 2:00 p.m. that afternoon.

"Her son never came to visit. In fact, Mrs. Henderson told me one time that she hadn't seen her son in quite some time. I saw him go in the house around 2:00 p.m. and I waved to him but he didn't acknowledge me. Come to think of it, her daughter hasn't come around much either. Apparently, there was some dispute of her will. Those kids were upset because Mrs. Henderson wanted to leave all her money to her poodle Pookie," the neighbor said.

Mrs. Henderson was a very wealthy widow. She lived meagerly but had millions of dollars in bank accounts and investments. She was survived by her two grown children, Katherine and William, who lived nearby.

Detective Summers decided it would be a good idea to question Mrs. Henderson's children. He called them into the station the next day. They arrived together.

"William, your mother's neighbor said she saw you at your mother's house Saturday at 2:00 p.m. Is that correct?" asked Detective Summers.

"Yes, I stopped by for a visit. I felt bad because I hadn't visited her in a long time. Since she was getting on in years, I felt I needed to visit her more. I stayed until around 5:00 p.m., then went to the grocery store before I went back home."

"Katherine, where were you that evening?"

"I was at home all day until 6:00 p.m., then I went to the Milford-Miami Township Branch Library and checked out a couple of books. I came back home immediately after that."

Detective Summers suspected Katherine to be the killer, why?

Need a Clue? Katherine's timing is off.

Evaluation

Count the number of contest entries to determine the number of participants.

Collection Tie-In

- Mysteries
- True crime
- Short stories

Alternative Approaches

Get a Clue is the perfect type of passive program to take online. Post each week's mystery on the library's website with a basic form asking for the solution and contact information. The contest could also be an ongoing feature in a library newsletter. Publish a different mystery each issue and direct respondents to submit their answers by e-mail or through an online form.

Resources

Mystery Digest, "Two Minute Mysteries," http://www.mysterydigest.com/two-minute-mysteries-cat/two-minute-mysteries/ (cited November 8, 2011).

MysteryNet, "Solve-it," http://www.mysterynet.com/solveit/ (cited July 20, 2011).

Get a Clue @ the library

... and solve the MYSTERY!

Use your best detective skills, come up with a solution, and you'll be entered in our **"Get a Clue @ the library"** contest. Each week, during the first four weeks of October, there will be a new mini-mystery for you to solve. You can start anytime because the contest lasts the entire month. The more mysteries you solve, the more chances you have to win the prize! Pick up an entry at any branch or at our website **www.clermont.lib.oh.us**.

- Check our website for mystery links
- Pick up a mystery author bookmark

...is Mystery Month

(contest is for 18 years & older)

CLERMONT COUNTY PUBLIC LIBRARY

Figure 3.1 Get a Clue program flyer. Courtesy of Clermont County Public Library and the author.

From *Librarian's Guide to Passive Programming: Easy and Affordable Activities for All Ages* by Emily T. Wichman. Santa Barbara, CA: Libraries Unlimited. Copyright © 2012.

Mystery Theme Contest

Lots of people love a good puzzle, and Judy McAloon of Prince William Public Library System (VA) has been offering them to her patrons for the better part of five years. Each month, Judy picks "a theme that can be logically deduced from the covers of books" that she displays in her library. For example, if the theme is "Mt. Rushmore presidents," there will be something on the cover of each book displayed that references George Washington, Thomas Jefferson, Theodore Roosevelt, or Abraham Lincoln. Patrons are challenged to identify the mystery theme, and one person with the correct answer wins a prize. Judy has built a core group of puzzle devotees who try their hands at her contests every month; see if you can do the same!

Make It Happen

1. Begin by choosing a mystery theme for your display. Many of the themes that Judy has used are given in the following section. For additional ideas, consider browsing visual dictionaries, since they are typically organized by subject. You might also subscribe to Fiction_L, a readers' advisory listserv, or search the listserv's archives. Fiction_L members regularly build booklists on a wide variety of topics that may provide theme ideas.

2. Determine what types of clues will fit your theme and develop a list of related keywords. The answer to the mystery should always be on the cover of the book. If the theme is "Man," you could use books with pictures of men on the cover (*The Irresistible Henry House* by Lisa Grunwald), books by authors whose names includes the word man (Henning Mankell), and books with man in the title (*Ambush of the Mountain Man* by William W. Johnstone). If the theme is "Olympic Medals," find books featuring the words gold, silver, and bronze. You might pick *The Princess Bride* by William Goldman (clue in author's name), *What Comes After Crazy* by Sandi Kahn Shelton (the cover of one edition is primarily silver), and *The Bronze Horseman* by Paullina Simons (clue in title).

3. Locate appropriate books for the display. Use the list of keywords developed to search the library's catalog for both titles and author names containing those words. Clues tied to cover art may be more challenging. Try browsing the stacks or posting a description of what you're looking for on Fiction_L. If you chose to display nonfiction materials, make sure that the book's subject is different from the contest theme. For example, if the contest theme was "Flowers," you could display *The Complete Idiot's Guide to Genealogy* by Christine Rose, but not a book on flower identification or gardening. Whenever possible, pick attractive, high-interest books. You're not only creating a program but also a display, and it's an opportunity to market the library's collection.

4. Select a prominent area for the display where it will be exposed to a lot of patron traffic. Based on the quantity of materials found relating to the theme, decide how many books to have on display at any given time. Judy typically has out 10 items. If the theme is reliant on multiple clue keywords, as with the "Olympic Medals" theme, then it is important to ensure that each keyword is part of the display at all times.

5. Create an entry form for participants wanting to take a guess at solving the puzzle. Ask what the patron believes the theme for the month is, and request his or her name and contact information.

6. Offer a prize for one person chosen randomly from all of the correct respondents. At Judy's library, the Friends group provides a $10.00 gift certificate to a local bookstore.

7. Launch the program by setting up the display, posting a sign explaining the contest (Fig. 3.2), putting out the answer forms and pencils, supplying an entry box, and giving notice of the prize. Judy sometimes provides participants with a hint if the theme is particularly difficult or if there is an alternative answer that the clues might also imply. When she used "Olympic Medals," she posted an advisory that the theme was not "Metals."

Sample Display Themes and Keywords

Chess pieces—king, queen, rook, bishop, knight, pawn

Four tastes—bitter, sweet, sour, salty

Words that sound like a letter of the alphabet—pea, cay, you

Car and truck models—Focus, Dakota, Ram, Wrangler, Beetle

First names of presidents' wives—Michelle, Laura, Hillary, Barbara, Nancy

Occupations—archer, baker, smith

Parts of the body—head, hand, lip, rib

Red—burgundy, crimson, maroon, ruby, scarlet

Crops—wheat, rye, corn, soybeans

Words that rhyme with "art"—start, cart, Bart, heart

American cities—Boston, Chicago, Madison, Austin, Charlotte, Buffalo

Weather—cold, sunny, rain, snow, ice, hot, pressure

Dog breeds—bloodhound, shepherd, terrier, beagle, collie

Fractions—tenth, eighth, sixth, fourth, quarter, half

Palindromes—radar, kayak, level, civic, Eve, Hannah, noon, mom

Family members—dad, father, sister, grandpa

Measurements—pound, inch, meter, cup, megabyte

Solar system—sun, moon, Pluto, Earth, Mars

Famous ships—*Arizona, Beagle, Bismarck, Bounty, Cole, Constitution, Endurance*

Months—April, May, June

Sports terms—ball, hoop, catch, kick, net, score

Green—chartreuse, emerald, forest, hunter, jade, kelly, lime, mint, olive

Double letters—good, mamma, tell, weed

Royalty—Elizabeth, Caroline, George, Louis

Card games—blackjack, bridge, fish, hearts, memory, poker, rook, solitaire, spades, war

Magazine titles—*Time, Gardening, Cosmopolitan*

Music terms—beat, cadence, canon, duet, encore, harmony, key

Dog days—dog, puppy, dog breeds, day, names of the days of the week

Last names of actors and actresses—Smith, Diaz, Willis, Stiller, Farrell, Bullock

Trees—oak, ash, maple, pine, sequoia

Directions—north, south, east, west, left, right, up, down, above, below, beside

Gemstones—sapphire, diamond, opal, jade, garnet, turquoise

Drinks—milk, tea, coffee, ale, Crush, julep, Mug, Heineken, Sam Adams

Evaluation

Determine the number of people who participated in the contest by counting the number of entries. Judy advises that participation can vary greatly, depending upon the difficulty of the chosen theme. If holding the contest several months, consider rotating easy themes with difficult ones as a way of maintaining interest.

Alternative Approaches

In many ways, it would be easier to run this program online instead of with a physical display. You never have to worry about running out of books, and it's OK if you can only find a couple of titles representing a particular clue. Use cover images or a list of titles, and post them on your website. If only providing titles and authors, limit yourself to clues found in the words. These contests would be a great reoccurring feature for a library blog, with patrons submitting their guesses through comments.

Resources

Morton Grove Public Library's Webrary, "Welcome to Fiction_L!," http://www.webrary.org/rs/flmenu.html (cited July 20, 2011).

Mystery Theme Contest

How good are you at puzzles? There is a theme tying together all of the books in this display. The theme can be identified by studying the front covers of the books, but has nothing to do with their actual content. Make your best guess and see if you can be the correct respondent to win a prize! This is an ongoing contest, with the answer and the winner from the past month, revealed at the start of each new month.

Figure 3.2 Sign explaining how to participate in the Mystery Theme Contest.

Whodunit?

Each summer, visitors to the Marion Public Library (OH) get to uncover the primary suspect in a fictional crime. For several years, the Children's Department staff, led by Barbara Moore, has created mysteries tied to the annual summer reading theme. Employees dress up as suspects, have their pictures taken, and each week a new clue is posted eliminating one of the potential perpetrators. Summer reading participants are encouraged to study the clues and photographs to determine which miscreant committed the offense. This popular program is loved by children and parents alike. As Barbara says, "Children get a great feeling of mastery when they can cross off a suspect."

Supplies

- Costumes
- Props
- Digital camera

Make It Happen

1. Start by designing a mystery. It can be as simple as, "Who stole item X?" This activity can be done at any time of the year, but doing it in conjunction with summer reading provides a built-in theme for the mystery. One year, the Marion Public Library summer reading topic was pirates, so the mystery was, "Who stole the map to the buried treasure?" A luau-themed program another year was accompanied by the mystery of "Who stole the apple from the pig's mouth at the luau?"

2. Decide how long the program will run. One character and one clue will be needed for each week of the program.

3. Think about how to create characters appropriate to the mystery. If the offenders are pirates, what kinds of costumes and accessories should they be dressed in? Write clues based on visual cues that will be found in the photographs. Each clue should eliminate one person in the series of images, so it is important to plan the order in which the clues are presented. As illustration, clues developed by Becky Dutton for Marion Public Library's pirate mystery are given in the following section.

4. Once each image has been planned, find some people willing to have their photographs taken and dress them in their costumes and props. If you have a hard time talking your coworkers into this endeavor, consider asking members of a library teen group or local theater association to pose for you.

5. To flesh out the mystery and add to the fun, make up names for the characters and write a brief alibi for each.

6. Create a poster for each suspect that includes a photograph, name, and alibi. Posters should be printed in color (Fig. 3.3–Fig. 3.4).

7. Create a handout for participants that states the mystery, provides instructions, and includes small images of each suspect. Marion Public Library prints this information in the summer reading packet that each child receives.

8. Kick off the mystery by hanging all of the character posters up in random order. Each week of the program, post one clue. Leave all clues up the entire length of the activity so that visitors can fully participate regardless of when they start the program.

9. Once the program has concluded, hang up a poster confirming the identity of the culprit (Fig. 3.5).

Sample Clues for a Pirate Mystery

Someone said the thief keeps both eyes on the treasure. (Eliminates a suspect wearing an eye patch.)

The thief always wears something on their head. (Eliminates a suspect without headgear.)

The thief left all 10 fingerprints at the scene. (Eliminates a suspect with a hook.)

The thief was armed and dangerous. (Eliminates a suspect without a weapon.)

Someone said the thief loves tropical birds. (Eliminates a suspect without a bird.)

The click-clack of women's shoes was heard running from the scene. (Eliminates a male suspect.)

The thief is happy to have gotten away with the crime. (Eliminates a frowning suspect.)

The thief kept the map out of sight. (Eliminates a suspect displaying a map.)

The clanking of jewelry was heard at the scene. (Eliminates a suspect not wearing jewelry.)

The thief doesn't like to read. (Eliminates a suspect holding a book.)

Evaluation

The staff at Marion Public Library view the mystery game as a fun, supplemental activity and don't track participation. If you chose to do so, the easiest methods would be to offer a small trinket to everyone who solves the mystery or to ask participants to turn in their completed handouts at the end of the program in return for an entry in a prize drawing.

Collection Tie-In

- Mysteries
- Materials related to the Whodunit? theme (pirates, Hawaii, etc.)

Alternative Approaches

One year, when the summer reading theme was bugs, Becky Dutton of the Marion Public Library Children's Department took a different approach to providing visitors with a puzzle. Close-up photographs were taken of different items in the library, and a multiple-lens effect was applied to each, simulating an insect's view of the world. Participants were challenged to identify the mystery objects. Becky called the program A Bug's Eye View (Fig. 3.6).

1.

Admiral Mean Stubble

"Don't speak to me about being a thief, ye scurvy dogs! Ye know I was locked in me private quarters sharpening me sword."

Figure 3.3 Admiral Mean Stubble (aka Barbara Moore), one of the suspects in Marion Public Library's pirate mystery. Courtesy of Marguarite Markley.

8.

Privateer Molly Lindsey the Thieving

"You think this map is stolen? It is me own map that I got from a coloring book. I be a good colorer."

Figure 3.4 Another possible perpetrator: staffer Marguarite Markley by day, pirate Molly Lindsey the Thieving by night! Courtesy of Marguarite Markley.

Figure 3.5 Final poster revealing that the true culprit was the nefarious pirate portrayed by staff member Whittney Mahle. Courtesy of Becky Dutton.

Figure 3.6 Program display for Marion Public Library's bug-themed puzzle challenge, A Bug's Eye View. Courtesy of Becky Dutton.

Chapter 4

Scavenger Hunts

If you're trying passive programming for the first time and you need to justify the effort with high participation rates, you'd do well to plan a scavenger hunt. While there's never any guarantee with programming, scavenger hunts tend to be very popular, particularly with children. Scavenger hunts are also appropriate if you're looking for an intergenerational program. These activities are perfect for families; kids can do the searching, while older siblings or adults help with reading instructions and completing answer sheets.

From a staff perspective, the real benefit I find in scavenger hunts is that they can be used to direct traffic through the library. Want people to discover your collection of children's music CDs or see the new couch in your reading area? Hide a clue nearby! Catch that Gnome! works particularly well for this purpose. Consider planning a scavenger hunt as part of a larger event, such as a holiday celebration or an open house. April Fools' Challenge and Find the Pickle! are two examples. I've heard from several libraries that do passive programming in conjunction with summer reading programs, which is a great way to drive participation. Letterboxing at the Library and Coded Message Scavenger Hunt are programs that can keep kids busy during weekly library visits all summer long.

April Fools' Challenge

The best April Fools' Day jokes are those that brighten the day with humor while not causing major inconvenience or embarrassment. One year, the Clermont County Public Library (OH) hosted a Wacky Day at each of its 10 branches. Staff members at the various locations dreamed up 10 wacky ways to modify their libraries for the day and challenged visitors to identify them all. This sort of activity encourages patrons to explore the library in more depth than they normally might. Best of all, from a staff perspective, redecorating the building in preparation for this program equals the opportunity for a bit of library-sanctioned high jinks.

Make It Happen

1. Determine when and for how long to host this program. Any day could be a Wacky Day, but it's fun to plan this event for April Fools' Day. If you do chose to celebrate April 1, will you set up the program for that day only, or allow it to run the entire week, so that more patrons can enjoy your efforts?

2. Depending upon the size of your building, determine how many visual jokes to set up. Place gags in a manner that will require participants to walk through the entire facility. Consider positioning the wacky items next to materials and services that you're eager to make library patrons aware of. Not all of the day's visitors will want to participate in the hunt for wackiness, so when planning the gags, make sure that they don't disrupt access to library services. Get creative and have fun in planning the jokes. Several examples are given in the following section.

3. Create posters explaining what's going on and inviting patrons to find all of the wacky items in the library (Fig. 4.1). Since this is a short-term program, and to minimize confusion, consider putting a display about the April Fools' Challenge right inside the front door. Instructions should tell participants how many items there are to identify. Supply paper and pens. Have people list all of the gags and bring their completed lists to staff. Reward participants with a small prize such as a piece of candy, bookmark, or pen. Be sure to create a cheat sheet for staff that lists all of the wacky items hidden around the building.

Sample Jokes

Display out-of-season holiday decorations—Christmas trees, pumpkins, etc.

Make a display of books with all of the back covers facing forward.

Using disposable dishes, set up a table to look like dinner is about to be served.

Fill display cases with something totally unworthy of display, such as cleaning products.

Make balloon faces or animals and perch them on shelves.

Put out some lawn chairs in the reading area.

If the staff doesn't normally wear uniforms, have everyone dress in matching clothing.

Rotate books on slatwall displays so that they are upside down.

Swap signs for items that are visually quite different, for example, trade signs for graphic novels and DVDs.

Put out empty flower vases at the reference desk.

Cover the signs on the bathroom doors with pictures of animals for which the differences between males and females are obvious, such as lions or cardinals.

Evaluation

Determine the number of participants by counting the number of prizes distributed.

Collection Tie-In

- April Fools' Day books
- Joke books
- Humorous fiction

April Fools' Challenge

Look around!

Do you see 10 W@CKY things?

If you can find them all, you'll win a prize!

Paper and pencils are available at the Information Desk. If you think you've found all 10 wacky items, bring your list to the desk to prove you're not an April Fool!

Figure 4.1 April Fools' Challenge program poster.

Catch That Gnome!

This was my first program to feature Mr. Gnome, and it was one of my most successful ever. At the time, my library had introduced several new services and I was looking for a creative way to make our users aware of them. I photographed the gnome next to the new items and created a scavenger hunt that sent patrons searching the building to locate all of the places Mr. Gnome had hidden. This program is perfect for directing visitors to library features that might otherwise go unnoticed.

Supplies

- Digital camera

- Mascot—The mascot doesn't have to be a gnome. Consider a stuffed animal, doll, or small statue. If your library has an official mascot, use it!

- Prize—My prize was a gnome, just like the one I'd used in the photographs. The prize can be anything, but it's fun to make it a copy of the mascot.

Make It Happen

1. Identify a handful of items in the library that you want to draw your patrons' attention to. Place the mascot next to these items and take a picture. In my program, I took pictures of Mr. Gnome with a chess set in the Teen Area, on the Friends of the Library book sale shelf, with the literacy kits, by the defibrillator, near the children's computer, and on the "time out" chair in the Children's Area. To make the scavenger hunt a bit harder, compose the photographs so that they only display part of the item patrons need to locate. For example, instead of taking a picture that shows an entire computer, take one that shows only the mouse.

2. Blow up the photographs and print them in color. Make a poster or display featuring the photographs and inviting participants to identify the places the mascot has been hiding (Fig. 4.2).

3. Create an answer sheet on which participants can identify the places they think the mascot was hiding. The ideal answer sheet will include small black-and-white images of each of the photographs next to the corresponding answer spaces. If offering a prize, don't forget to ask for contact information (Fig. 4.3).

4. Launch the program by setting up a display that includes the photographs, answer sheets, pens, an entry box for completed sheets, and the prize. I always like to stick a colorful "Win Me!" sign on the prize.

Evaluation

Determine the number of participants by counting the number of completed answer sheets.

Alternative Approaches

Instead of running the program over a short period of time, featuring all of your photographs at once, post the images one at a time in the library's newsletter or on its website. Invite readers to identify where the photographs were taken. Prizes can be awarded to the first correct respondent or a randomly selected winner. This approach works best for a library that has only one facility.

Figure 4.2 Create a display using all of the photographs. The poster text reads: "Catch that Gnome! There's a gnome loose in the library! Can you tell where he's been? He'll come home with one lucky person who can discover the location of his hiding places."

Catch that Gnome!

There's a gnome loose in the library! Can you tell where he's been?

Where is he?

Where is he?

Where is he?

Where is he?

Where is he?

Where is he?

Name: _____   Phone Number: _____

Figure 4.3 Catch That Gnome! answer sheet.

Coded Message Scavenger Hunt

The Children's Department at Ela Area Public Library (IL) has found great success with a passive program developed by Barb, a longtime employee, combining two sure-to-appeal activities: scavenger hunts and coded messages. For approximately the last 12 years, she has developed a code in which each letter of the alphabet is assigned a symbol. The letters and their accompanying symbols are printed on small pieces of paper and hidden throughout the department. With a symbol key in hand, kids have to find each letter and record it on the key. Every week, a new secret message is posted and participants have to use their key to decode it. Children's librarian Liz reports that the program generates great excitement, with "teams of kids racing around the Children's Department, announcing excitedly when they find a clue." During the eight-week 2010 summer reading session, 40 to 140 children participated in the program each week, with a total of 575 entries submitted over the period!

Make It Happen

1. Pick out 26 easily distinguishable symbols, one for each letter of the alphabet. Copyright-free clip art works well for this purpose. At Ela Area Public Library, symbols are chosen to correspond to the year's summer reading theme. Because the activity is so popular, the library sometimes revives it in September for Talk Like a Pirate Day.

2. Using the images chosen, create an answer key. Each symbol should have a blank space nearby where the accompanying letter can be recorded. Brief program instructions should also be included on this handout (Fig. 4.4).

3. Make clues by printing each symbol and the letter it equates on a three-by-five-inch piece of paper. Since the clues will be posted around the library for an extended period of time, consider printing them on cardstock for added durability.

4. Decide how long to run the program and write one question for each week. The answer to the question will be the coded message (Fig. 4.5). The trivia used in the questions can follow the theme used for the symbols. Create a poster for each week that states the question in plain text and the answer written in code. Make answer sheets for each week that include the question and a space for each letter of the answer. Be sure to have a place for participants to record their names and phone numbers (Fig. 4.6).

5. Get ready to launch the program by hiding the clues. To keep the activity from being too difficult, it is best to hide the clues only in the Children's Department. Finding all 26 clues will be sufficient challenge for most kids; so "hide" the clues in easy-to-spot locations.

6. Set up a staging area for the program. Ela Area Public Library uses a bulletin board and table. Hang up the weekly question, have answer keys and entry forms available, and supply pens and an entry box (Fig. 4.7).

7. Swap out the questions and answer sheets weekly, but use the same code for the entire length of the program. Once children have filled in their answer keys, encourage them to hang onto the keys so that they can use them to decode the answers to upcoming questions.

8. Each week, give away a small prize to one participant, as doing so will help sustain interest in the program.

Evaluation

Count the number of entry forms to determine the number of participants in the program.

Collection Tie-In

- Fiction and nonfiction about codes

- Fiction and nonfiction about spies

- Mysteries

- Materials relevant to the theme chosen for the program's symbols and questions

Deep Blue Read
Scavenger Hunt Answer Key

All the clues are hidden in the Children's Department. Look for the blue clues!

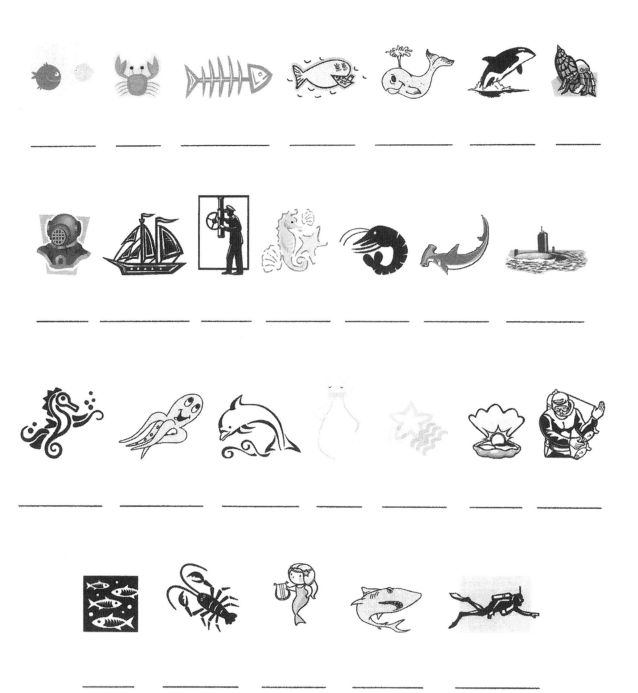

Figure 4.4 Scavenger hunt answer key with graphics tied to Ela Area Public Library's 2011 summer reading program theme, Deep Blue Read. Courtesy of Barb.

Question: There are over 120 varieties of _ _ _ _ _ _ _. A well cared for one can live 15 to 25 years.

[Answer: goldfish]

Figure 4.5 Example question with the answer written in code. Courtesy of Barb.

Deep Blue Read Scavenger Hunt, Week 2

Write in your answer below and check back next week for a new question!

There are over 120 varieties of ___ ___ ___ ___ ___ ___ ___ ___.

A well cared for one can live 15 to 25 years.

Name: _____

Phone number: _____

Figure 4.6 Each week of the program will require its own entry form due to the changing questions. Courtesy of Barb.

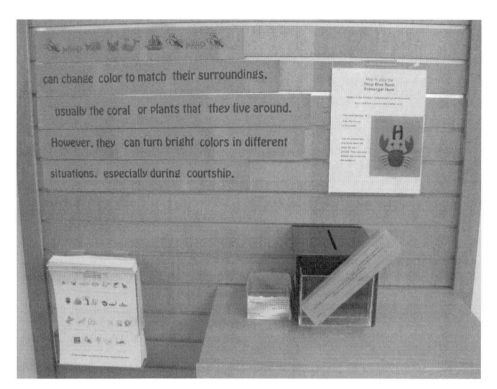

Figure 4.7 The scavenger hunt program set up includes the coded message, instructions, answer keys, entry forms, an entry box, and pencils. Courtesy of Liz.

Find the Pickle!

If you've spent any time in Christmas shops, you've probably come across at least one selling glass pickle ornaments, packaged with a legend explaining that it's an old German tradition to hide a pickle on a Christmas tree. Children search for the pickle, and the first to find it receives an extra gift. The origins of this "legend" are vague, and online forums are full of Germans claiming no knowledge of this "tradition," but it's a fun idea all the same. Certainly many of the Christmas traditions familiar to Americans, including glass ornaments, have their origins in Germany. Every year, my library has a Holiday Open House, typically offering crafts, games, food, and a performance. One year, our theme was Holidays Around the World, and for an activity, I hid images of giant pickles around the library for attendees to find. Make the activity more educational by posting facts about verified Christmas traditions from other countries with each pickle.

Make It Happen

1. Make large pickles, at least one foot long, after deciding how many to hide around the library. If there's an artist among your coworkers, have him or her draw some pickles for you. If not, you can find clip art pickle images.

2. Assign a country to each pickle and research its Christmas traditions. Write a few sentences about each country, highlighting an interesting feature of its celebrations. Several examples are given in the following section. A fact about each country will be hung with each pickle, so make sure the text is large enough to be read from the hiding place. Consider adding a map or image of the country's flag to each write-up (Fig. 4.8).

3. Create a quiz with one question about each country featured. The quiz can be multiple-choice or fill-in-the-blank, so long as participants can answer each question by having read all of the country facts (Fig. 4.9).

4. In my experience, scavenger hunt programs are an easy sell, but you might want to add an incentive to drive participation. Consider distributing a small prize to every person who finds all of the pickles and is able to complete the quiz. The prize could be a piece of candy, a sticker, or bookmark. Alternatively, give out entries for a chance to win a grand prize, maybe a pickle ornament!

5. Decide how long to run the program. The Find the Pickle activity can either be part of a larger holiday event or can last throughout the holiday season. Many countries celebrate Epiphany as the final event of the Christmas season, so you might consider having the program conclude 12 days after Christmas.

6. Just before the start of the program, hide the pickles throughout the library. The country facts need to be displayed next to the pickles, so be sure to choose spots that have sufficient room for both.

7. Launch the program with instructions, copies of the quiz, pencils, and an example of what the hidden pickles look like. Enhance the appearance of the display with pictures of Christmas being celebrated around the world, a world map, or flags of foreign countries.

Sample Country Facts

Across *Australia* on Christmas Eve, Carols by Candlelight festivals are held in parks. People gather to sing Christmas carols and donations are collected for charity.

Chile's version of Santa Claus is called Viejo Pascuero (Old Man Christmas). He travels by sleigh and reindeer but enters homes by way of a window. Children leave out their shoes for Viejo Pascuero to fill with small gifts.

On Juleaften (Christmas Eve), families in *Denmark* gather for a large dinner that traditionally includes rice porridge. Hidden in the porridge is a single almond. Whoever finds the almond wins a small treat, often a marzipan pig.

In *England*, children send letters to Father Christmas by throwing them into the fire.

Christmas celebrations in *Ethiopia* are primarily religious, with gift exchanges limited to minor items such as clothing. A game similar to field hockey, called genna, is played only on Christmas Day.

At Christmas, children in *Italy* write letters to their parents promising good behavior in the coming year and sharing their love.

As part of Christmas Eve festivities in *Mexico*, blindfolded children vie to break open a piñata by hitting it with a long stick. The piñata is a clay jar in the shape of an animal and is filled with treats.

The most predominant symbol of Christmas in the *Philippines* is the parol, a five-pointed star lantern. During the holiday season, towns hold lantern festivals with prizes for those who build the most impressive lights.

Participating in the "Urn of Fate" is a Christmas tradition in *Spain*. Names are placed in an urn and drawn out in pairs. The two people chosen are to become friends in the coming year.

In *Sweden*, the Christmas season begins on December 13 with St. Lucia's Day. Dressed in a white robe with red sash and head wreath with seven lit candles, the family's eldest daughter serves coffee and buns to family members in bed.

Evaluation

Count the number of completed quizzes to determine how many people participated in the program.

Collection Tie-In

- Christmas materials
- Winter holiday stories from around the world
- Materials on winter holiday traditions from around the world
- Fiction by non-American authors
- Memoirs by non-American authors

Alternative Approaches

Just as we strive to provide balanced collections, a library celebrating the holiday season should acknowledge the traditions practiced in its community. If you're not recognizing celebrations such as Hanukkah and Kwanzaa with other activities, then add information about these events to the pickle search. Instead of sharing information about Christmas celebrations around the world, you could share explanations of the different ways the winter holidays are celebrated throughout the United States.

Resources

Bowler, Gerry. *The World Encyclopedia of Christmas*. Toronto: McClelland & Stewart Ltd., 2000.

Crump, William D. *The Christmas Encyclopedia*. Jefferson: McFarland & Company, Inc., Publishers, 2001.

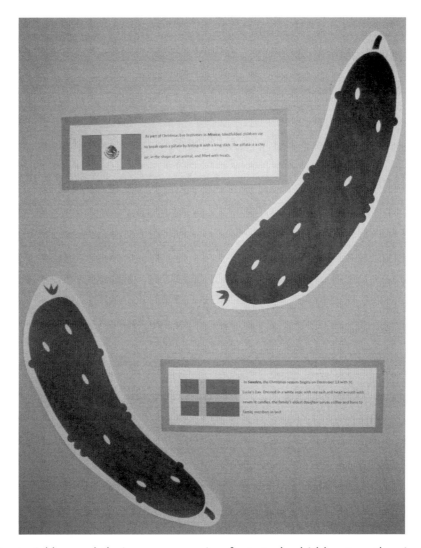

Figure 4.8 Giant pickles and their accompanying facts to be hidden together in the library.

FIND THE PICKLE!

Tradition claims that German families once hid a pickle ornament on the Christmas tree and that the first child to find the pickle on Christmas morning was rewarded with an extra gift. While there is debate on whether or not this has ever been a true German custom, or if it is simply a story invented to sell ornaments, there are many real holiday traditions from around the world that you can learn about.

There are 10 pickles hidden in the library. By each pickle you will find a fact about how the Christmas season is celebrated in a different country. If you read all 10 facts, you will be able to answer the questions on this quiz. Turn your completed quiz in at the Information Desk for a reward!

1. In Chile, Viejo Pascuero enters homes to deliver presents by way of a:

   (a) Door   (b) Window   (c) Chimney   (d) Garage

2. What is hidden in the porridge that is traditionally eaten on Juleaften in Denmark?

   (a) An almond   (b) A ring   (c) A miniature pig   (d) A raisin

3. How do English children send their letters to Father Christmas?

   (a) By mail   (b) By balloon   (c) By fire   (d) By e-mail

4. What is a parol?

   (a) A pastry   (b) A lantern   (c) A flower   (d) A song

5. What country is known for its Carols by Candlelight festivals?

   (a) Spain   (b) Ethiopia   (c) Australia   (d) Sweden

6. What do Italian children write in their Christmas letters?

   (a) Promises of good behavior   (b) All of their wrongdoings
   (c) A wish list of presents   (d) New Year resolutions

7. What word describes a clay jar filled with treats?

   (a) Corazón   (b) Tarro   (c) Abuela   (d) Piñata

8. What country's Christmas Day celebrations include the "Urn of Fate?"

   (a) Denmark   (b) Australia   (c) England   (d) Spain

9. What color robe do girls in Sweden wear on St. Lucia's Day?

   (a) Blue robe with red sash   (b) Red robe with white sash
   (c) White robe with red sash   (d) White robe with blue sash

10. What game is similar to the Ethiopian game of genna?

   (a) Field hockey   (b) Football   (c) Basketball   (d) Polo

---

Figure 4.9 Find the Pickle quiz.

Letterboxing at the Library

Letterboxing is a hobby in which people follow a set of clues in order to find a hidden box. Each box holds a logbook and a rubber stamp, which is often a hand-carved work of art. Letterboxers each have their own stamp, which they imprint into a box's logbook to record their discovery of it. Letterboxers then imprint the stamp from the letterbox into their own personal logbook.

Maureen Brehm, a patron of the Easton Area Public Library (PA), "fell in love with letterboxing as a way to get out, hike, use your brain, exercise, think, and have fun as a family." Realizing that some letterboxes are hidden indoors, and wanting to share her hobby with others, Maureen approached librarian Katie Cardell about starting a letterboxing program at the library. Working together, Maureen and Katie developed a modified letterboxing program to coincide with summer reading. Each week, a new box was hidden in the library for children to discover if they accurately followed a set of clues. Interest in the program far exceeded expectations, and letterboxing has become an annual part of the summer reading program at Easton Area Public Library. The second year the program was offered, there were more than 1,000 participants, and several local child-care centers began making weekly visits to the library just for this activity.

Not only is the library's letterboxing program fun, but it has practical outcomes too! Katie found that following clues helps children to develop counting and directional skills. She notes that, "Over eight weeks, we really notice improvement in the way children read and follow step-by-step instructions. It also serves as a great way to help younger children (and sometimes not-so-young children) learn the difference between left and right, forwards and backwards, up and down."

Supplies

- Small metal boxes—The box must be able to stay closed when hung on the underside of a shelf. The small tins that some breath mints and cough drops are sold in work well.

- Magnets—The magnet needs to be small enough to be glued to the bottom of the metal box, but strong enough to hold the box to the underside of a shelf.

- Rubber stamps—Either purchase premade rubber stamps or design your own with a stamp-making kit. Kits are available online and at art supply stores.

- Ink pads

- Binder rings

- Prizes—Inexpensive novelty toys (temporary tattoos, bouncy balls, etc.) and candy are well received by children at Easton Area Public Library.

Make It Happen

1. To determine the amount of supplies needed and how many letterboxes to make, decide how long to run the program and how often new boxes will be hidden. Easton Area Public Library puts out a new box each Monday during its eight-week summer reading program. Putting out new boxes on a regular basis encourages repeat library visits.

2. Assemble all of the supplies needed for each letterbox. Spray paint metal boxes and attach a magnet to the underside of each. Create a logbook for each box. This can be as simple as cutting sheets of paper small enough to fit the box, punching a hole in the corner of each, and holding them together with a binder ring. Katie recommends making a few extra boxes and logbooks, as the originals occasionally become misplaced during the program. Have extra pages on hand to expand the logbooks if they

become full. Make or buy a rubber stamp for each box. Katie designs stamps that correspond with the year's summer reading theme (Fig. 4.10).

3. Establish guidelines for the program. What ages are invited to participate? Easton Area Public Library opens the program to summer reading participants, although teens and adults express interest in the activity also. Children need to be able to read in order to complete the program independently. With the assistance of an adult companion, letterboxing is suitable for children as young as five. At Easton Area Public Library, children are allowed to find each box as many times as they like but are only permitted one prize per box. If a child has difficulty finding the box, he or she is asked to try two times. If still unsuccessful, a staff member will assist the child.

4. Decide where the letterboxes will be hidden and write a clue sheet for each. Clues should include directions such as: Stand with your back to the water fountain, Take 5 steps forward, Turn right, Take 3 steps forward, Look under the shelf with books about hamsters, and so on. Make the clues for finding each new box progressively harder as the program advances; you might even consider using misdirection to make the discovery more challenging. Children at Easton Area Public Library had to follow nine clues to find the first letterbox, but by week eight, they had to follow 51 clues in order to locate the final box. Example clues that Katie developed for Easton Area Public Library are given in the following section.

5. To kick off the letterboxing activity, Easton Area Public Library held a program called Learn to Letterbox. The summer-long project was explained to families, and children had the opportunity to make their own stamps from craft foam. Holding a similar event at your library would be a good way to promote this passive program, in addition to standard methods like in-house advertising (Fig. 4.11), event calendars, and press releases.

6. Once the program is underway, visitors participate by first stopping at the service desk to pick up a clue sheet. When the box has been found, the person brings it back to the desk. A staff member lends the participant a stamp to print in the logbook, along with the person's initials and the date. The person is then asked to replace the box in its original hiding place before returning to choose a prize. In practice, this program is a variation on traditional letterboxing, as most participants will not have their own personal stamp and logbook.

7. When multiple letterboxes will be in play at the same time, Katie recommends color coding all of the supplies for each box. For example, for the first letterbox, make the covers of the logbook, the clue sheets, and the envelope holding the corresponding rubber stamp purple. Choose a different color for each letterbox that follows.

Sample Short List of Clues for Locating a Letterbox

Start at the front of the youth services desk.

Turn around and face the back wall.

Take 1 side step to the left.

Take 10 giant steps forward.

Take 4 side steps to the right.

Take 4 giant steps forward up the aisle.

Turn right.

Count 4 shelves down from the top.

Do you see the books about pet fish? Look underneath the shelf.

Is something hiding there?

Sample Long List of Clues for Locating a Letterbox

Start at the front of the youth services desk.

Turn right.

Take 4 steps forward.

Turn right.

Take 4 steps forward.

Take 3 side steps to the right.

Take 7 steps forward.

Take 1 side step to the left.

Take 8 steps forward.

Turn left.

Take 3 steps forward.

Take 7 side steps left.

Take 10 steps forward.

Turn right.

Take 3 steps forward.

This isn't right! Wrong way!

Start over at the front of the youth services desk.

Turn around and face the back wall.

Take 11 steps forward.

Take 3 side steps to the left.

Take 9 steps forward.

Turn right.

Take 7 steps forward.

Take 4 side steps right.

Turn left.

Take 6 steps backward.

Turn right.

Take 3 steps forward.

Turn right.

Take 6 steps forward.

Turn left.

Take 6 steps forward.

Do you see all the Dr. Seuss books?

Wrong way again.

Turn right.

Turn right.

Turn right.

Take 8 steps forward.

Turn left.

Take 5 steps forward.

Take 2 sidesteps to the left.

Take 13 steps forward. Almost there!

Take 3 side steps to the right.

Take 3 steps forward.

Turn right.

Take 4 steps forward.

Turn left.

Take 3 steps forward.

Find the spot where the *Percy Jackson* books would be. The author's last name is Riordan.

Look under the shelf directly below where those books would be.

Is something hiding there underneath that shelf?

Evaluation

Distributing small prizes encourages participation in this program, but if only children receive gifts, counting the number of items distributed is not the best way to track participation. Parents and other caregivers are sure to assist children with the program and should be recorded as participants. Keep a sheet for tracking statistics at the service desk, and each time someone asks for a clue sheet, record the number of people in the group.

Alternative Approaches

Consider setting up a permanent letterbox in the library and posting clues for it on one of the letterboxing websites. Maureen has established a Harry Potter letterbox at Easton Area Public Library. A copy of one of the books from the series is jacketed and labeled to look like library material, but inside, the center is carved out to hold a stamp and logbook.

Geocaching is an activity closely related to letterboxing, with hidden boxes containing logbooks but no stamps. Geocaches are found using GPS coordinates, and participants are encouraged to record their experiences finding the boxes online. Set up a geocache at your library and you might just have people visiting your facility for the very first time.

Resources

Books

Cameron, Layne Scott. *The Geocaching Handbook: The Guide for Family Friendly, High-Tech Treasure Hunting*. Guilford, Conn: Falcon, 2011.

CQ Products (Firm). *It's a Treasure Hunt!: Geocaching & Letterboxing*. Waverly, IA: CQ Products, 2007.

Gillin, Paul, and Dana Gillin. *The Joy of Geocaching: How to Find Health, Happiness and Creative Energy Through a Worldwide Treasure Hunt*. Fresno, CA: Quill Driver Books, 2010.

Hall, Randy. *The Letterboxer's Companion: Exploring the Mysteries Hidden in the Great Outdoors*. Guilford, Conn: FalconGuides, 2011.

Peters, Jack W. *The Complete Idiot's Guide to Geocaching*. Indianapolis: Alpha Books, 2009.

Websites

Atlas Quest, http://www.atlasquest.com (cited July 21, 2011).

Geocaching, http://www.geocaching.com (cited July 21, 2011).

Letterboxing North America, http://www.letterboxing.org (cited July 21, 2011).

Figure 4.10 A letterbox with corresponding logbook and rubber stamp. The logbook covers and stamp envelope are both blue. Courtesy of Katie Cardell.

Figure 4.11 One method the staff at Easton Area Public Library uses for promoting programs such as Letterboxing at the Library is to decorate end panels with homemade posters. Courtesy of Katie Cardell.

Chapter 5

Get Creative

Many libraries host craft programs and visits from performance artists. If these events are well attended at your library, then it's not a stretch to imagine that passive programs requiring patrons to use their creativity will be well received also. Your library may already have a coloring or craft table set up in the Children's Area. These stations have their value, particularly in keeping children engaged while their caregivers complete their business at the library. But, if you're going to spend money on supplies and time on preparing crafts, why not channel those efforts into developing activities that piggyback off your library's larger programming efforts? The LEGO Display can kick off a new LEGO Club for children, and Chain Calendars can help count down the days until a major program begins, drumming up enthusiasm along the way. Activities like Masquerade can be a part of your summer reading program, while Star Garlands could be a welcome addition to a wintertime openhouse event.

Chain Calendars

When I was little, nearly every major event was anticipated with the help of a chain calendar (Fig. 5.1). I would create a picture appropriate to the upcoming festivity, be it my birthday, Christmas, Halloween, or the last day of school. Next, I would count out the days remaining until the Big Day, and make a paper chain with a link for each. With the chain attached to the picture, the calendar was complete, and the countdown would commence. Hanging on my bedroom wall, each morning would begin with a link torn from the calendar's chain, and a clear reminder of how much time remained until the long-awaited event.

A chain calendar is a great tool for helping children to mark the passage of time. At the library, such a calendar can be used to drum up enthusiasm for a major program, such as summer reading.

Supplies

- Picture-making supplies—Provide either a coloring sheet with an image appropriate to the upcoming event or materials for children to make their own designs. Potential supplies include crayons, markers, glue, scissors, glitter, cotton balls, yarn, tissue paper, etc.

- Construction paper

- Stapler

- Staples

- Calendar—A monthly calendar is best. Repurpose a wall calendar, or print only the required months using the calendar templates typically found in word processing software.

Make It Happen

1. This program obviously needs to be planned to coincide with an important occasion. You might choose to count down to a holiday, a major anniversary, or a community event. Creating chain calendars can be a way to promote major library programs, like summer reading, author visits, and special performances.

2. Plan to start the program about 25 days in advance of the event and to finish it about six days prior. A chain calendar that is much longer than 25 links will become unwieldy, while one much shorter than six links won't be satisfying to use.

3. Each calendar needs a base sheet that the chain can be attached to. The sheet should be a picture that relates to the event. If promoting summer reading, you might make a beach reading–themed coloring page (Fig. 5.2). The reverse side of the paper can include details about the program. Alternatively, skip the coloring sheet and simply provide construction paper, craft supplies, and maybe a few examples to prompt creativity. Counting down to Halloween, the base sheet might be a large jack-o'-lantern cut from orange paper, with various black paper shapes that can be glued on to create faces. Possibilities are numerous, depending upon available supplies.

4. Cut strips of construction paper that will be used to make the chain links. Each strip should be one inch wide and approximately eight to nine inches long. Pick paper colors that compliment the event, such as red, pink, and white for Valentine's Day. Kids will enjoy choosing from a variety of colors and creating patterns with the links.

5. Find or make calendar pages that show all of the days during the one or two months that the program runs. Clearly mark on the calendar the day being celebrated. Participants will be counting the days in order to determine the number of links needed to make their chain calendars.

6. Write instructions for making and using a chain calendar (Fig. 5.3). Making the calendar involves decorating the base sheet, determining how many links are needed, assembling the chain, and attaching the chain to the sheet. Using the calendar is as simple as hanging it up at home and removing a link each day.

7. Make up a few sample chain calendars and hang them around the library, particularly where children will see them. Include signs directing people to the craft table to make their own calendars. Don't forget to remove a link each day!

8. Set up the craft at a table that allows plenty of space to work. Provide either a coloring sheet or picture-making supplies, along with lots of paper strips. A stapler is needed to close each chain link, so be sure to have lots of staples. Post instructions and the relevant calendar pages. Display one of the chain calendar examples close at hand.

Evaluation

Track participation by counting the number of coloring sheets provided. If not using a coloring page, and instead creating pictures from a variety of supplies, try to include one item that would be used in all the pictures. For example, each jack-o'-lantern would require one piece of orange paper.

Collection Tie-In

- Materials related to the special event
- Craft books
- Books about calendars, clocks, and time

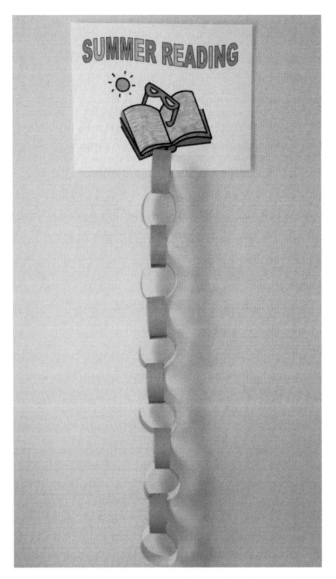

Figure 5.1 A completed chain calendar counting down the days until the start of summer reading. Printing details about the program on the reverse, such as its run dates, how to register, and a list of prizes will encourage participants to follow through and get involved.

Figure 5.2 A simple design that could be the base coloring sheet used to create a calendar counting down to the launch of a summer reading program.

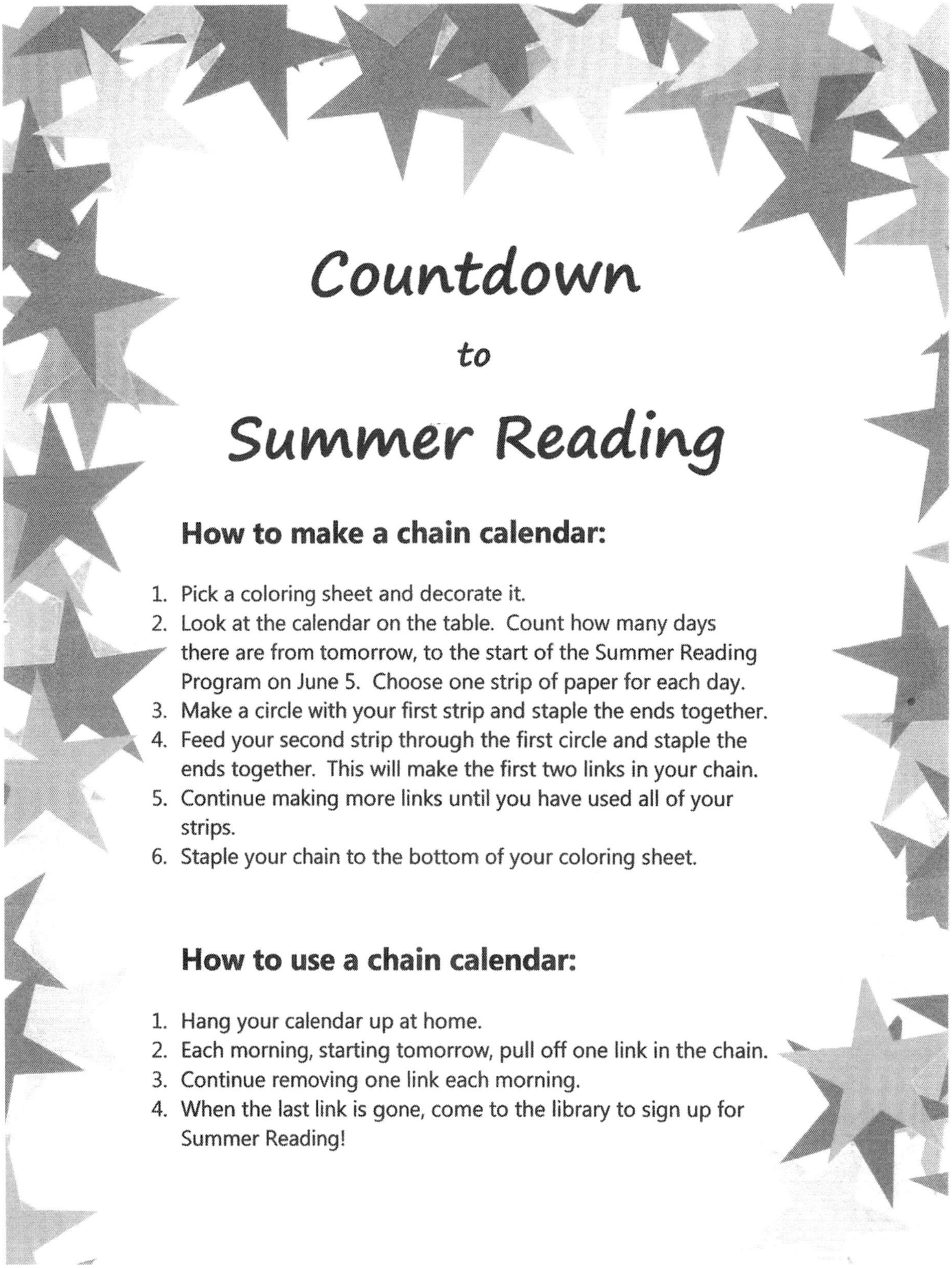

Countdown

to

Summer Reading

How to make a chain calendar:

1. Pick a coloring sheet and decorate it.
2. Look at the calendar on the table. Count how many days there are from tomorrow, to the start of the Summer Reading Program on June 5. Choose one strip of paper for each day.
3. Make a circle with your first strip and staple the ends together.
4. Feed your second strip through the first circle and staple the ends together. This will make the first two links in your chain.
5. Continue making more links until you have used all of your strips.
6. Staple your chain to the bottom of your coloring sheet.

How to use a chain calendar:

1. Hang your calendar up at home.
2. Each morning, starting tomorrow, pull off one link in the chain.
3. Continue removing one link each morning.
4. When the last link is gone, come to the library to sign up for Summer Reading!

Figure 5.3 Instruction sheet describing how to make and use a chain calendar.

LEGO Display

LEGOs are a perennially popular construction toy. From time to time, we hear news of some ambitious builder who has erected a massive scale model of a monument, stadium, vehicle, or animal. These hobbyists are limited in their designs only by scope of imagination and quantity of available bricks. LEGO clubs are now popping up in libraries across the country. Kelly Clark of Clermont County Public Library (OH) tapped into this trend by inviting library users to make their own LEGO creations and display them at the library. This event generated much enthusiasm and would be a great way to build an audience for ongoing LEGO programming.

Make It Happen

1. A LEGO display program is a two-month project. The first month is needed for advertising the event and giving participants enough time to build their objects. Submissions are displayed during the second month.

2. Look around your building and determine what locations can be used to safely exhibit the LEGO creations (Fig. 5.4). Display cases and countertops are obvious choices. Maybe some of the highest bookshelves throughout the library are empty and could be used for display. Space within the children's area would be particularly appropriate.

3. Based on the amount of display space available, determine what the size limitations should be for each LEGO project. Kelly required that submissions be able to fit inside a one-foot cube.

4. Create a handout or bookmark explaining how the program works, what the rules are for submissions, and how people can register. At Clermont County Public Library, all ages were welcome to participate, but builders had to supply their own LEGOs and ensure that their creations complied with size restrictions.

5. Launch the program a month before the submission deadline with a poster and the instruction sheets. Displaying a large, eye-catching LEGO creation will help with promotion (Fig. 5.5). Be sure to put out any LEGO books owned by the library!

6. As LEGO designs are submitted for display, the library may want to require participants to sign a release of liability form. While individual pieces are unlikely to break, a completed design may be fragile and difficult to move. If creations are displayed in the open, they should be positioned out of easy reach, as there will almost certainly be people who will want to touch and examine the objects more closely.

7. It shouldn't take a lot of incentive to find library users eager to participate in this program, but offering a prize never hurts. This is supposed to be a fun, creative activity, so avoid issues of unfairness or hurt feeling by awarding any prize randomly.

Evaluation

Participation is determined by the number of submissions received. If multiple people work together on a single creation, count individuals separately.

Figure 5.4 A selection of LEGO creations on display in a locked case.

Figure 5.5 Promotional set up seeking participants for LEGO Display program.

Masquerade

Summer reading programs provide the perfect opportunity for self-directed programming. Participating families visit the library on a regular basis to pick up books and log their reading accomplishments. Hot temperatures, long evenings, and freedom from the burden of homework encourage visitors to linger. If your reading program is built around a theme, providing supplemental programming is practically a requirement. A few years ago, with a summer reading program called "Be Creative @ Your Library," Amanda Harris and Theresa Wiseman of New Albany-Floyd County Public Library (IN) decided to include a mask-decorating kit among the prizes awarded to children who completed the program. Kids were encouraged to decorate their masks and bring them back to the library to be displayed and entered in a contest. Abby Johnson, the library's Children's and Outreach Services Manager, provided extensive detail on the implementation of the program and reported that the mask contest was a huge success, with some 200 children participating!

Supplies

- Undecorated half masks—Likely to be white in color and made of plastic or cardboard with an elastic band, these masks cover the eyes.

- Mask-decorating supplies—Staff at the New Albany-Floyd County Public Library chose to include in each kit a selection of stick-on jewels, feathers, and a paintbrush. Alternatives abound: stickers, pompoms, ribbon, foam shapes, tissue paper, etc.

- Resealable zipper bags

- Prizes—Donated books in good condition are a cost-free option.

Make It Happen

1. Decide when to offer this program and how much time to give participants to decorate and submit their masks. You'll need a large area to display all of the entries, so be sure to choose a time when there will be a month's worth of space available following the entry deadline. Certainly the mask contest can be held independently of a summer reading program, but distributing the supplies as a prize is an innovative way to encourage high levels of participation.

2. Determine what materials will be included in each kit (Fig. 5.6). Many decorative items will be choking hazards, so allow age warnings to guide the decision on what the minimum age should be for participation in the contest. Each kit will need an entry form asking for name, grade, and phone number. Also include a sheet of instructions listing where and when to submit masks, judging guidelines for the contest, and a note about choking hazards. Packing all of the kit materials into resealable bags is a perfect volunteer job.

3. Most families will probably want to craft their masks at home, but some may ask if they can do so at the library. Consider setting up a craft table with glue and other supplemental materials where children can work on their masks.

4. If distributing the masks as a summer reading prize, make sure all staff is trained to promote the mask contest when handing out the kits. If running the contest independently of summer reading, be sure to take standard promotional steps such as creating a program poster, making a display of decorated masks, and hand-selling the kits.

5. As masks are returned to the library, collect them in a central location. Assign each mask a number and attach it to the front where contest judges will easily be able to view it (Fig. 5.7). Note the assigned

mask number on the corresponding entry form and file the forms away until it is time to contact contest winners.

6. When the entry deadline has passed, create a gallery of all the masks. At the New Albany-Floyd County Public Library, this meant stapling each mask to large bulletin boards in the programming room. Divide the masks into judging categories based on age, such as preschool through kindergarten, first through second grade, and so on (Fig. 5.8). Select a panel of judges to pick winners in each age category. Judges could be Friends of the Library members, local art teachers, or community figures. Abby notes that when the winners were announced, there were parents who commented on the fact that some children obviously had help in designing and constructing their masks. Combat these concerns by stating in the contest instructions whether parental assistance is permitted. Alternatively, skip the judging and award prizes by drawing random names.

7. Get even more mileage out of the mask program by hosting a masquerade party to announce the winners, award prizes, and give the children an opportunity to model their masks.

8. Once you take down the mask gallery, hang onto the masks for a few months so that they can be returned to any child that comes in asking for them.

Evaluation

Count the number of decorated masks submitted to the library to determine how many people participated in the program. If hosting a masquerade party, attendance at that event can be recorded separately.

Figure 5.6 A selection of completed masks demonstrating the many design variations possible, even with a limited selection of kit supplies. Courtesy of Abby Johnson.

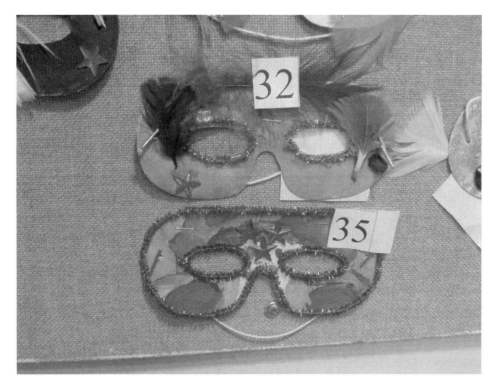

Figure 5.7 When displayed, masks were assigned numbers for use in judging. Staff at Albany-Floyd County Public Library stapled patron entry forms to the back of each mask for easy identification. Courtesy of Abby Johnson.

Figure 5.8 Masks organized by age and displayed on bulletin boards in the Albany-Floyd County Public Library programming room. Courtesy of Abby Johnson.

Star Garlands

Several years ago, I attended a program on making Christmas decorations from recycled greeting cards that was hosted by the Hamilton County Park District (OH). One craft involved creating a garland of paper stars, and I was pleasantly surprised to see just how attractive the resulting product was. With clear instructions, this is a craft your patrons can make without supervision, and they will love it! This is by far the most popular passive program I have ever offered, with 253 library users completing their very own star garland. So appealing was the project that several other branches in my library system also chose to offer this craft.

Supplies

- Greeting cards—Preferably cards with winter holiday images.
- Twine—Yarn and ribbon are suitable alternatives, but a natural-colored twine compliments the style of this craft.
- Scissors
- Staplers—Miniature or "pocket" staplers with a narrow profile are essential. A regular stapler is too large to easily manipulate when making this craft.
- Staples
- Hole punch

Make It Happen

1. Unless you just happen to have a massive supply of greeting cards on hand, this program requires planning a year in advance. I have always found library users to be extremely generous, especially when asked to donate something that will help them to declutter their homes. The best time of year to obtain greeting card donations is immediately after Christmas. For a few weeks on either side of the holiday, put up signs around the library requesting that patrons bring in their holiday cards or any other greeting cards they'd like to dispose of. The last time I asked for donated cards was the winter of 2006/2007, and there are still a handful of patrons who bring me their Christmas cards every year! Only the fronts of the cards are needed for this craft, so if people want to cut the backs off the cards, where messages are generally written, that is perfectly acceptable.

2. Assume each person who makes a star garland will want to make at least 10 stars, and you'll have an idea of how many cards you need. Cards must have a flat, rectangular front in order to work for this craft. Depending upon the amount of time you have, you may want to sort out and dispose of unsuitable cards as donations come in. Find a nice, large, sturdy box to collect the donations.

3. Decide when and for how long to run the program. December is the obvious time, but I would suggest starting the week of Thanksgiving, since that is when many people begin decorating their homes.

4. Make promotional posters inviting library visitors to participate in the program. Assemble paper stars and hang garlands around the library. Individual stars can be hung as ornaments.

5. Create an instruction sheet for making star garlands modeled after the photographs and instructions depicted in Fig. 5.9 through Fig. 5.14. Including photographs is essential if this craft is to be largely self-directed. Still, staff will receive occasional questions on how to make the stars, so be sure to give your coworkers a quick tutorial. When I did this program, I placed the instructions on a table and attached them by completely covering them in clear tape. This prevented the instructions from

disappearing or being torn. Most likely, at least a few patrons will ask for a copy of the instructions to take home, so consider keeping copies at the reference desk.

6. Decide how to handle the distribution of twine. If your library has success leaving craft materials unattended, precut the twine and leave it at the craft table. Three to six feet is a good length for a garland. If craft supplies tend to disappear, then leave instructions for participants to come to the reference desk, where they can choose how long a piece of twine they want to cut.

7. Launch the program by setting up the craft table in a prominent area. Consider pushing a couple of tables together, as there is a good chance you'll have multiple participants working simultaneously. Tape instructions to the tabletop. Make scissors, mini staplers, extra staples, and a hole punch available. You may want to use long pieces of yarn to tie these tools to the table legs as a means of encouraging them to stay put. Place the box full of cards on the table. I made a garland the length of the box circumference and taped it around the edge, so that crafters would have a model to look at. This activity creates a lot of scraps, so have garbage cans close at hand.

8. There are many things that can be done with leftover cards when the program ends. Save them for another year, or offer them to coworkers at different libraries so that they can do the craft also. My library has a patron who cuts bookmarks from the covers of greeting cards. These make for an extremely popular freebie.

Evaluation

The easiest way to track participation in this program is to count the number of lengths of twine that are distributed, as each piece represents one garland.

Collection Tie-In

- Holiday craft books
- Origami and paper craft books
- Books on crafting with recycled materials

Figure 5.9 Pick a card to use in making your star. You only need the front of the card. Tear or cut off the back.

Figure 5.10 Fan fold your card into eighths. Make sure that when you lay your card down on the table, your folds look exactly like they do in this picture.

Figure 5.11 Squeeze the fan folds together and bend them in half.

Figure 5.12 Cut off the tip of each end at a 45-degree angle. This will make the points for your star. Be sure your cuts look like the ones in this picture.

Figure 5.13 Open up your fan folds so that they make a complete circle. Your card will now begin to look like a star. On each side of the star, bring together the ends and staple them together on the back side. Look at this picture to see the location of the staples.

Figure 5.14 Flip your star over. It should look like this picture. Punch holes at the tip of two adjacent points. Cut a piece of twine ranging from three to six feet long. Make as many additional stars as you like. String the stars on the twine to complete your garland.

Chapter 6

Exchanges

The public library is a wonderful example of the community pooling its resources for the greater good. At many libraries, this pooling of resources goes beyond tax dollars. Community experts share their knowledge and skills in programs, volunteers provide literacy touring and computer assistance, while multiple agencies might even share a facility. Exchange programs allow your patrons to share their resources in another way. Regardless of what is being swapped, be it craft supplies, jigsaw puzzles, or greeting cards, exchange programs work when one participant brings in an item she is no longer able to use and trades it for an item left by a different participant that suits her needs better. Recycling in action! Tracking participation in exchange programs can be very difficult, but they're worth your time because they help build community and goodwill. Look around your house, think about different hobbies, consider things that are used by everyone, and you'll find yourself with more exchange ideas. What about swapping plants, seeds, or bulbs? How about used books, DVDs, or CDs? Maybe recipes, coupons, or travel brochures? What things can you think of to trade?

Craft Supply Swap

A perennial problem for most serious crafters is the overwhelming size of their "stash." Ask an artist or crafter you know about how much house space she has devoted to her supplies, and with a little prodding, she'll probably confess to, at minimum, an overflowing closet. Many crafters are willing to thin their collections for a good cause or the chance to swap materials. Introduce these folks to the many great resources our collections have to offer them by turning your library into a temporary site for exchanging craft supplies.

Make It Happen

1. A month before launching the program, begin advertising so that participants will have time to think about what items they might be willing to exchange. Make posters and flyers stating how long the event will run and what sorts of items can be swapped (Fig. 6.1). I recommend making the Craft Supply Swap a month-long activity and suggest that materials for trade include craft kits and unused supplies in good condition and of substantial quantity.

2. Consider whether there are any types of supplies that cannot be accepted. You may want to avoid paints and adhesives for safety reasons or because of their spill potential. Expect participants to trade anything from rubber stamps to yarn, patterns, glitter, and embroidery hoops. You may find that patrons want to bring in large quantities of material, particularly of fabric and yarn, but don't necessarily want to take home an equivalent number of items. If space is an issue, limit contributors to three or four pieces per person.

3. Pick a prominent area in your library to set up the Craft Supply Swap. You'll need a space with plenty of room for all of the items brought in for exchange, and you'll want a spot that's highly visible. If at all possible, launch the program with a few craft supplies already on display. Raid your own personal craft stash for these items, ask your coworkers for donations, or check the library's craft closet for odds and ends.

4. Decide in advance what you will do with any leftover materials, as you may be asked about this by participants. Quite possibly, remaining items will be useful for future library programs, so invite your programmers to look the materials over before disposing of anything. Unclaimed items that are not wanted by the library can be donated to a local thrift store.

Evaluation

Monitoring the number of participants in a Craft Supply Swap can be challenging unless an enticement is offered that requires people to check in with library staff. Each swapper could be offered an entry in a drawing for a prize. Alternatively, individuals might be given a small, prepackaged craft kit to take home. Avoid incentive expenses by inviting participants to come to the desk for a special bookmark. A list of Dewey numbers for popular crafts would be a welcome resource for many (Fig. 6.2).

Collection Tie-In

- Craft books—Choose a theme such as introductory guides for learning new crafts or books full of holiday projects.

- Art instruction books—Painting, sketching, cartooning, etc.

- Instructional arts and crafts DVDs

- Resources on starting a crafting business

Figure 6.1 Craft Supply Swap program poster.

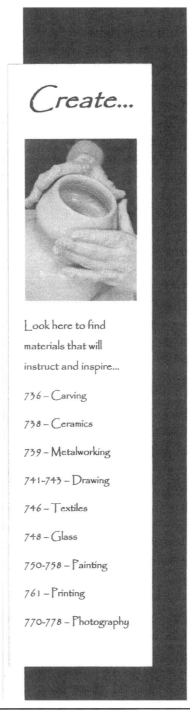

Create...

Look here to find
materials that will
instruct and inspire...

736 – Carving

738 – Ceramics

739 – Metalworking

741-743 – Drawing

746 – Textiles

748 – Glass

750-758 – Painting

761 – Printing

770-778 – Photography

Figure 6.2 Bookmark that can be distributed to swappers as a means of evaluating participation.

Puzzle Exchange

Gaming programs have become a staple in many libraries. Perhaps your library has added an evening of board games or has started a bridge club, Scrabble club, or chess club. Your collection may even include video games that are available for checkout. Expand upon this theme by starting a collection of jigsaw puzzles that circulate on the honor system. Unlike a favorite board game that is played time and again, people who build puzzles are always on the lookout for their next challenge. Starting a puzzle collection is a perfect example of recycling: Old items repeatedly become new each time they are borrowed by a different user, and all participants save money while continuing to enjoy their hobby. I have run a self-sustaining puzzle exchange at my library for several years. In the first year of the program, I had more than 800 recorded checkouts and lots of positive feedback!

Supplies

- Jigsaw puzzles—There are many ways to obtain puzzles at no cost. Try any of these methods:

  ◦ Coworkers—Ask staff members if they have any puzzles they'd be willing donate for your program.

  ◦ Patrons—Over the years, library users have been my primary source of puzzles. Several hundred have been donated to date. Put up a sign in the lobby or at the service desk soliciting donations, and you're bound to have plenty of puzzles in no time.

  ◦ Senior Facilities—Visit almost any senior facility and somewhere you'll find a table with a half-completed jigsaw puzzle. Get to know the activity directors and ask if they'd be willing to give some of their old puzzles to the library. Your puzzle exchange will become a resource for them, allowing the facilities to continue providing puzzles while diverting their puzzle funds to other programs.

  ◦ Commercial Donations—Any store with a toy department is likely to sell puzzles. Ask stores in your community to donate a few puzzles to start your collection.

- Printable address labels

Make It Happen

1. Plan to run the puzzle exchange on the honor system. The goal is for this program to require very little in the way of staff or supply costs. Assume that some puzzles will be permanently "borrowed," that pieces will be lost, and that boxes will be damaged. Focusing on developing a steady stream of donations will make it easy to weed the collection of damaged or underused items.

2. Consider the population of your service area when deciding how many puzzles need to be collected before starting the program. For a mid-sized library, try to have at least 30 jigsaw puzzles.

3. Create some lending rules for the puzzle exchange and print those rules on a label that can be affixed to the bottom of the puzzle box (Fig. 6.3). Does your library system have multiple branches? If so, is every branch creating a puzzle collection? Do you want your puzzles to float between branches or to be returned only to the location where they were borrowed? Do you have an outdoor return box? I can guarantee you don't want someone throwing a 1000-piece puzzle into it! The label I use with my puzzle collection contains the following statements:

   - Please return puzzle when completed.

   - Inform staff if pieces are missing.

- Return to Milford-Miami Twp. Branch.

- Return to puzzle shelf.

- Do not place in outdoor return box.

4. Pick a location to house the puzzle collection; the more visible the better (Fig. 6.4). If you do not have prime real estate to devote to puzzles, consider displaying them prominently for a few months with signage noting their future location.

5. Launch the program by displaying the puzzles with instructions explaining how the exchange works (Fig. 6.5). Include a solicitation for additional donations. If you plan to use a check-out sheet, put it on a clipboard with an attached pen (Fig. 6.6). Draw attention to the new collection by putting a puzzle out on a table for patrons to build. Put a sign on the table that says, "Enjoying this puzzle? Borrow a different puzzle to take home with you. Visit our Puzzle Shelf [insert location]."

6. If you're lucky, you may find that the amount of jigsaw puzzles donated to the library exceeds the available space to house them. If you are so fortunate, weed the puzzle collection frequently, adding new donations to keep things fresh. If you still have too many puzzles, sell some in your used book sales.

Evaluation

Creating a check-out sheet for the puzzle exchange is the easiest way to monitor its use. I put a number on the bottom of each puzzle box and asked users to record the number of the puzzle, the day it was borrowed, and the day it was returned. Following an honor system, some checkouts are bound to go unrecorded, but this method will give an idea of how much use the collection is receiving.

Figure 6.3 Back of puzzle box with puzzle number, rules sticker, and branch label.

Figure 6.4 Puzzle collection with sign and check-out sheet.

Jigsaw Puzzles

These puzzles are for you to check out on the honor system.
Just take one home and return it to this shelf when you have completed it.

Please note on the check out sheet which puzzles you borrow.

If you find a puzzle that is missing a significant number of pieces,
please let a staff member know. Puzzles can only be returned to the
Milford-Miami Township Branch Library and *should not* be
placed in the outdoor return box.

If you would like to donate any puzzles that are in good condition,
please give them to a staff member.

Figure 6.5 Puzzle Exchange sign. Courtesy of Clermont County Public Library.

PUZZLE CHECK OUT

Write the number of the puzzle you're checking out (found on the back of the box) and the date you check
the puzzle out. When you return the puzzle, make a note under the In Date column.

Puzzle #	Out Date	In Date

Puzzle #	Out Date	In Date

Figure 6.6 Puzzle Exchange check-out sheet.

Winter Holiday Card Exchange

If you're a person who annually sends out holiday greeting cards, you've probably wondered about what to do with the leftover cards invariably found in the bottom of the box. Do you save them for next year? Will people remember that you sent the same card two years in a row? Do you stockpile the cards for years and only send them to people newly added to your address book? While by no means a problem of earth-shattering proportions, the issue of leftover cards is yet another one of life's many dilemmas that can be solved by the library! Host a Card Exchange and invite patrons to bring in their unused winter holiday cards to swap for those left by others, and everyone will go home with the peace of mind that comes from knowing that they will not have sent the same card twice!

Make It Happen

1. When beginning to plan this program, check the calendar to see on which dates the winter holidays most commonly observed in your community fall. The dates for celebrations such as Hanukkah change from year to year. Schedule the card exchange to run the entire length of the holiday season. A mid-November through early-January timeframe is generally safe.

2. Decide on rules for the exchange. Can participants take home only one card for each card left behind, or can people take and leave cards indiscriminately? When I offered this program, my rules included this statement: "You may take one card for each card you leave." What I discovered is that people jump at any opportunity to clean out their houses, especially if they think that by doing so, they are supporting a good cause. So, if you find that there are more cards coming in than going out, you may choose to relax the one-to-one exchange rule.

3. Consider whether to offer a prize. Monitoring participation in exchange programs is difficult. One way to get a feel for the number of people who brought in cards is to offer each one an entry in a prize drawing. Since gift giving is a standard part of the holiday season, I awarded an attractive box of thank-you cards as a prize.

4. Write instructions for the exchange. Cards should be unused and swappers should be encouraged to only bring in cards that have envelopes. Provide rubber bands and ask that like cards are bundled together. If following the one-to-one exchange rule, be sure to make note. If offering a prize, give directions on how to obtain an entry form.

5. Keep the card exchange tidy and easy to browse by finding containers to hold the cards. Gift-wrapped lids from copier paper boxes work well and can be made to look festive (Fig. 6.7).

6. Ask coworkers and volunteers to bring in some of their leftover cards prior to the start of the program so that early participants will have some variety to select from. Before long, there will be more than enough cards on hand for staff members to pick out some new ones for themselves.

7. Launch the program with a poster (Fig. 6.8), instructions, cards from coworkers displayed in box lids, and rubber bands for bundling. If awarding a prize, include entry forms, an entry box, and display the prize prominently.

8. Don't despair if there are leftover cards after the program is complete. Consider picking out the cards that aren't holiday specific and saving them to send to library volunteers and supporters the following year. Cards can also be used in a variety of crafts, such as Star Garlands, which is featured in the previous chapter.

Evaluation

Tracking participation in a card exchange is challenging. The number of prize entry forms will give a suggestion, but when I hosted my exchange, I had reason to believe that many swappers declined to enter into the drawing. It may be more successful to position the exchange near a service desk and ask staff to keep track of the number of patrons observed taking part.

Collection Tie-In

- Card-making books

- Scrapbooking resources

- Holiday craft guides

- Books with ideas for homemade gifts

Alternative Approach

Offer a card exchange in any season by simply inviting patrons to swap all types of greeting cards. Blank cards, birthday cards, get well cards, anniversary cards, and sympathy cards are all options in addition to holiday cards.

Figure 6.7 Winter Holiday Card Exchange in progress with greeting cards available for trade on display.

Winter Holiday Card Exchange

Hesitant to send out your leftover holiday cards from last year? Participate in our greeting card exchange and snag some fresh cards. You're also entered into a drawing to win a box of **Thank You cards** when you participate.

November 15-December 31

During Library Hours • All Ages

MILFORD-MIAMI TOWNSHIP BRANCH • Clermont County Public Library
1099 State Route 131 • Milford, OH 45150 • 513-248-0700

visit us at www.clermontlibrary.org

Figure 6.8 Program poster for Winter Holiday Card Exchange. Courtesy of Clermont County Public Library and the author.

Chapter 7

Partnering with Outside Organizations

Partnering with an outside organization on a passive program is a good way to develop a new relationship or strengthen an existing one. From the public's perspective, working with other entities helps to reinforce the library's larger role in the community. Many of these partnership programs involve an element of charity and volunteerism, another source of goodwill. These types of passive programs are a prime opportunity for publicity, as the media may be more inclined to pick up a positive story featuring two or more institutions.

Both Crafting for Charity and The Spreading Cheer Project are crafting-based service programs. While likely to appeal to many patrons, these programs could particularly be beneficial to teens in need of service credit. Do You Recognize Me? taps into the community's collective memory to try and shed light on the people, places, and events in unidentified historic photographs. Meet the Milfords is a fun exchange program that invites multiple towns with the same name to learn about one another. Think about the different organizations in your service area, and you're sure to come up with some creative ways to partner with them for more passive programs.

Crafting for Charity

Working in libraries, I have been impressed by the generous natures and willingness to participate in volunteer activities that have been exhibited by so many of our users. I also know that there are lots of knitters, crocheters, and sewers out there in Libraryland. Harness both impulses by giving patrons a charitable outlet for their crafting habits. There are many established nonprofit organizations that make use of handmade items such as baby clothing, blankets, slippers, hats, and mittens. Pick a few of these charities, provide your users with instructions, give them some time to craft, and see how many good works they can produce!

Make It Happen

1. Pick two to four charities that accept handcrafted items. Make sure that your selection of charities provides opportunities for knitters, crocheters, and sewers. Consider picking charities that accept small items such as hats, as opposed to major items like afghans. Some charities require the donations to be shipped to their headquarters, while others have drop-off sites in your community. Consider how the donations will be delivered when choosing which charities to feature. In my program, the featured charities were: Care Ware (booties and bibs for babies), The Ships Project (slippers for soldiers and sailors), and The Snuggles Project (blankets for shelter animals). See the Resources section for assistance in choosing charities.

2. Decide how long the program will run. Participants need time to plan and complete their projects. Many will want to make more than one item. I found three months to be a good length of time.

3. Create a set of instructions for each of your charities. Most charities have specifications for the donations they accept. The charities may require that donations be made of specific materials, that they be made in certain sizes, and that the items are packaged following particular procedures. Include on your handouts the name of the charity, a description of the charity's mission, the charity's website, any requirements specified by the charity, and the due date by which donations must be dropped off at the library. Most charities provide patterns on their websites. Either refer patrons to these online patterns or provide printed copies (Fig. 7.1).

4. Launch the program by setting up a display announcing the project. Make sure you have plenty of handouts for each charity. If you aren't skilled in the fiber arts, draft a crafty friend to make up a few sample donations in advance. Displaying the samples draws attention to the program. If there's room, collect and store the donations in the area where the program is set up. Seeing the donation pile grow will encourage additional participation.

Evaluation

This program can be evaluated either by counting the number of individuals who participate or by counting the number of donations collected. Tracking the donations is easier and better represents the charitable impact of the program. If you choose to count individuals, have participants register for the program. Alternatively, offer a small incentive and use prize drawing entry forms to determine the number of participants.

Collection Tie-In

- Craft books and instructional films—Display materials that complement the charity projects.

- Volunteerism guides and manuals
- Volunteerism memoirs

Alternative Approaches

This program is easy to run simultaneously on the library's website, which will help in recruiting additional crafters. Simply post all of the instructions, provide links to the charity websites, and let participants know when and where to drop off their donations.

A mitten tree is an alternative approach to this program that is accessible to a wider audience, because both store-bought and handcrafted items can be donated. Generally associated with the winter holidays, a mitten tree can be tied in with other seasonal activities.

Resources

Charities

Afghans for Afghans, http://www.afghansforafghans.org/ (cited July 22, 2011). Blankets, sweaters, vests, hats, socks, and mittens for Afghanistan.

Care Wear, http://www.carewear.org/ (cited July 22, 2011). Clothing for babies.

Project Linus, http://www.projectlinus.org/ (cited July 22, 2011). Blankets for ill and traumatized children.

The Ships Project, http://www.theshipsproject.com/ (cited July 22, 2011). Hats and slippers for the military.

The Snuggles Project, http://www.snugglesproject.org/ (cited July 22, 2011). Blankets for shelter animals.

Books

Christiansen, Betty. *Knitting for Peace: Make the World a Better Place One Stitch at a Time.* New York: Stewart, Tabori & Chang, 2006.

Greer, Betsy. *Knitting for Good: A Guide to Creating Personal, Social & Political Change, Stitch by Stitch.* Boston: Trumpeter, 2008.

Macomber, Debbie. *Knit Along with Debbie Macomber: A Charity Guide for Knitters.* Little Rock: Leisure Arts, 2009.

Websites

Interweave Knits, "Knitting Charities: Knitting for a Better World," http://www.interweaveknits.com/community/charities.asp (cited July 22, 2011).

Lion Brand Yarn, "Charity Connection," http://cache.lionbrand.com/charityConnection.html (cited July 22, 2011).

Care Ware

Mission: Care Wear is a national organization of volunteers who make handmade baby items for hospitals. Items can be knit, crocheted, or sewn.

Website: www.carewear.org

Project: Sew bibs and booties to be worn by babies being cared for at Children's Hospital.

Instructions: Sew bibs and/or booties using cotton flannel, cotton knit, or terry fabrics. Sample patterns can be found at the website, or you may use your own. Do not use fabric softeners when washing the fabrics. Do not use buttons or any other swallowing hazards. Items should be packed in plastic bags, keeping booties together with safety pins. Drop off finished items at the Milford-Miami Township Branch Library before August 31.

Figure 7.1 Example text for a Crafting for Charity instruction handout.

Do You Recognize Me?

Historical societies are obvious partners for libraries as both deal with the organization and preservation of information while also having a focus on education. When I learned that the Greater Milford Area Historical Society (OH) is working to organize and digitize its photograph collection, I was told that their holdings include numerous unidentified photographs. The Society frequently partners with my library to present programs, so after hearing about this project, I saw an opportunity for a passive program. The best way to get those photographs identified is to show them to a large audience. What better place than the public library with its high traffic and locally based users? After displaying a variety of photographs for a month, the Society obtained several leads on the identities of the people, places, and events featured in the images. Those who didn't recognize any of the pictures still enjoyed seeing the historic hometown photographs.

Supplies

- Unidentified photographs
- Locked display cases
- Scanner
- Photo paper

Make It Happen

1. Contact your local historical society to see if they have any photographs in their collection that they would like the library's assistance in trying to identify. At this time, you might also talk to the society's representative about offering a historically themed program at the library to coincide with the display as a way of drawing attention to the project.

2. Determine how much space you have for displaying photographs, and have those constraints direct which images the historical society chooses for the program. Since the images are unidentified, the society may not know for certain geographically where they were taken. Despite this, every effort should be made to select images from your community, as those are the ones your patrons are most likely to recognize. Group shots and pictures of community events are particularly good choices to display, as the number of people likely to be familiar with those images increases (Fig. 7.2—Fig. 7.3).

3. Historical images from the society's collection could quite possibly be unique, irreplaceable objects, so the library needs to do its best to ensure that they are not damaged or stolen while being used for the program. Displaying the pictures in a locked case is ideal. If the pictures are to be displayed in an unsecured location, scan the images, print them on photo paper, and leave the originals safely at the society's headquarters. Even with a locked case, making reproductions is still a good choice if there is any concern about damage from light or other environmental factors.

4. When ready to display the images, label each one with a number. If library users know anything about the photographs, you want to be sure that information is received by the historical society. Make a form that asks for the number of the image that the person recognizes and a summary of what is known. Inquire also if the society can contact the person to discuss the picture further and request name and contact information (Fig. 7.4).

5. When the program begins, next to the display, set out the identification forms, pencils, and a box to collect the forms.

Evaluation

It's very difficult to track how many people look at a display, but you'll know how many attempted to identify a photograph by the number of identification forms completed.

Collection Tie-In

- Local history books
- Genealogy books
- Bookmarks for genealogy databases
- Photography books

Alternative Approaches

The library's website almost certainly receives many more hits than the website of the historical society. Establish a long-term partnership between your two organizations and feature a different unidentified photograph on the library's website weekly or monthly. Patrons will like seeing the pictures while the library helps in the effort to preserve the community's history.

Figure 7.2 A photograph of a large group of people has greater potential for being identified than an image of a single person. Courtesy of the Greater Milford Area Historical Society.

Figure 7.3 In this image, viewers might recognize either the building or the women. Courtesy of the Greater Milford Area Historical Society.

Do You Recognize Me?

Photograph Number: _____

What do you know about this photograph?

_____

_____

_____

Can the Historical Society contact you?

Name: _____

Phone Number: _____

E-mail: _____

Do You Recognize Me?

Photograph Number: _____

What do you know about this photograph?

_____

_____

_____

Can the Historical Society contact you?

Name: _____

Phone Number: _____

E-mail: _____

Do You Recognize Me?

Photograph Number: _____

What do you know about this photograph?

_____

_____

_____

Can the Historical Society contact you?

Name: _____

Phone Number: _____

E-mail: _____

Do You Recognize Me?

Photograph Number: _____

What do you know about this photograph?

_____

_____

_____

Can the Historical Society contact you?

Name: _____

Phone Number: _____

E-mail: _____

Figure 7.4 Photograph identification forms, with four fit to a page.

Meet the Milfords

Growing up, I had a number of pen pals living across the country and around the world. I enjoyed trading letters with my pen pals, swapping photos and postcards, while getting a glimpse of lives lived in different locales. In the back of my mind for years was the idea of doing some sort of pen pal–inspired library program, but I struggled with finding a practical way to implement it. My library is in a town called Milford, and one day someone mentioned having recently driven through another Milford in a different state. Surely, I thought, there must be more than two Milfords in the United States. After a bit of searching, I became aware of 10 other libraries situated in towns called Milford. Soon I was forming thoughts on how to partner with these libraries to develop some sort of exchange activity between the various Milfords.

The resulting program was Meet the Milfords, in which libraries from Connecticut, Iowa, Michigan, and Ohio participated. Patrons at each library drew pictures of their town and wrote letters explaining why it was special. Library staff took photographs and wrote profiles of their towns and libraries. All of these materials were exchanged among the participating libraries and used to create displays designed to introduce the communities to each other. Not only does this program encourage patrons to reflect on what makes their own town unique, but it also invites them to learn about locations they may never have heard of otherwise. As a programmer organizing this activity, you'll get the pleasure of meeting new colleagues and learning a bit about library activities in other systems.

Supplies

- United States map—Map should be large enough to pinpoint the location of each town. A laminated map is nice because you can use it for future projects.
- Three-ring binder
- Dividers

Make It Happen

1. Begin by searching for libraries located in towns with the same name as yours. This is easily done using an Internet search engine. You may need to be a bit flexible with the name, allowing for such variations as West Milford or New Milford. If your town has an unusual name, consider searching for some other common feature, such as county name, high school name, or location along a similar longitude or latitude.

2. Write a proposal letter to introduce yourself and explain the program idea. State that you are willing to provide digital copies of all of the materials needed for the program. Make it clear what the responsibilities will be for each participating library (promotion, printing handouts, collecting community information, and mailing packets). Ask libraries to inform you whether they are interested in participating in the exchange by a specific date. You should be able to find an e-mail address on most library websites for either the director or someone in charge of programming. Send your letter to this person.

3. Once you know which libraries will be participating, begin assembling the materials needed for the program. About a month before the activity begins, e-mail digital copies of the following items to each contact:

   - Poster—Create a poster for the program that the other libraries can use if they choose not to make their own publicity (Fig. 7.5). Be sure that it includes an invitation to return to the library to view the final display.

- Coloring Sheet—Design a coloring sheet that looks like a postcard (Fig. 7.6). Across the top write something like, "Greetings from . . ." or "Welcome to . . ." Give instructions to "Draw a picture of your town here."

- Letter—Create a form letter that older participants can use (Fig. 7.7). Give a few writing prompts such as, "My favorite thing about my town is . . ." or "I love my library because. . ."

- Instructions—Provide instructions on what each library needs to do to execute the program (Fig. 7.8). Include details about making copies of the poster and handouts, the dates that the program runs, gathering and assembling community information, instructions and a deadline for mailing the packets, and suggestions for creating a display of the materials from each town.

- Community Profile Template—To provide some consistency for the final display, create a template for each library to share information about its community (Fig. 7.9). Provide some prompts for writing about the community and the library. I ran the program in summer, so I also asked about seasonal activities.

- Contact List—Create a list of addresses and program contacts for each participating library.

4. When it's time to launch the program, set up at a table so that participants will have room to color and write. Make a display with a program poster and a map indicating the locations of the other towns. Put out copies of the coloring sheet and letter, along with crayons and pens. Supply a tray or box to collect the pictures and letters so that patrons don't take them home. If your library already has a coloring table, you might set the activity up there or put out a sign directing people to the program.

5. Before the active part of the program is finished, make sure that coordinators at each library are gathering their community information. Ask everyone to take three to five pictures each of their town and their library. Have them complete the Community Profile Template, providing a brief narrative about their town and library.

6. Once the period for collecting pictures and letters has ended, the program coordinators at each library should assemble packets to mail to each of the other participating libraries. The packets need to include a selection of completed coloring sheets and letters, a copy of the Community Profile, and labeled copies of all photographs. Encourage everyone to mail the packets within one week of completing the program.

7. Once the packets have arrived, create a display that showcases all of the materials collected. I hung up a large United States map, surrounded it with the photographs and information that each library provided, and ran lengths of yarn between each community's information and its location on the map. Also display the pictures and letters. If you don't have enough wall space around the map, you might put them in a binder for patrons to browse through. Plan on leaving the display up for a month or two (Fig. 7.10).

Evaluation

Count the number of completed coloring sheets and letters to see how many people participated at each library.

Collection Tie-In

- State books—Display books about the states participating in the program. This could include travel guides, state profiles, and setting-heavy fiction.

- Books about libraries

Meet the Milfords

Send your greetings across the country to library users living in other cities and towns named "Milford". Complete a coloring sheet or letter and we'll send it to another Milford library. Come back next month to see a display of the pictures and letters the other Milfords sent to us.

June 2011
All Ages

MILFORD-MIAMI TOWNSHIP BRANCH • Clermont County Public Library
1099 State Route 131 • Milford, OH 45150 • 513-248-0700

visit us at www.clermontlibrary.org

Figure 7.5 Meet the Milfords program poster. Leave information specific to your own library off the version you send to the other participating libraries. Courtesy of Clermont County Public Library and the author.

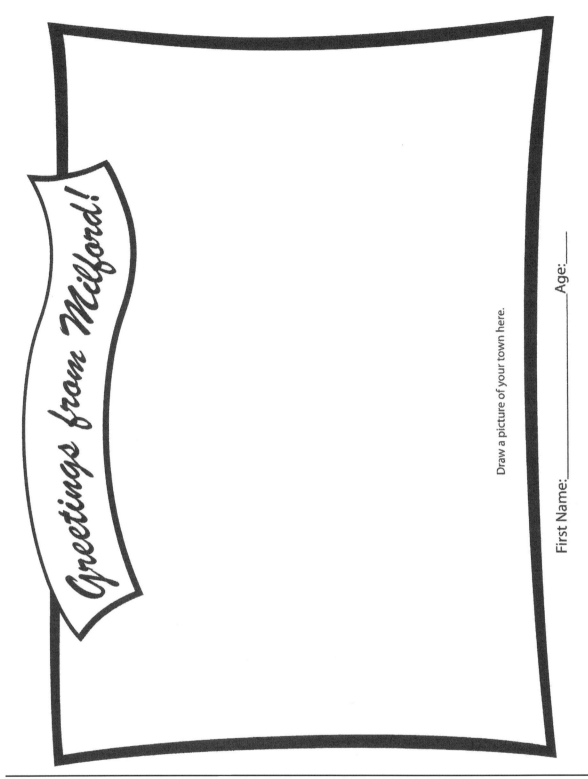

Figure 7.6 Coloring sheet designed to look like a postcard. Courtesy of Clermont County Public Library.

My favorite thing about my town is:

I love my library because:

First Name:_____Age:_____

Figure 7.7 Letter encouraging participants to share information about their town. Courtesy of Clermont County Public Library.

Meet the Milfords

Instructions

Publicity: Make copies of the included poster or create your own. Publicize the program through all of your normal channels.

Handouts: Make copies of the coloring sheet and the letter.

Launch the Program: Run the program June 1 – June 30. Make a display, set out the handouts, and include instructions. Advertise the fact that the materials from other Milfords will be on display in July and August.

Community Materials: Use the "Questions" document as a guide and create a document that talks about your community and library. Take 3-5 photos each of your library and your town. Label the photos on the front. Make three copies of all of the photos and the questions document. These materials will be included in the final displays, so use fonts large enough for people to read from a short distance.

Exchange Materials: After June 30, end the program and divide all of the coloring sheets and letters into three groups. Mail a packet to the other three participating libraries.   The packet should include: coloring sheets completed by your patrons, letters completed by your patrons, your responses to the questions document, and copies of all of your photos. Packets should be mailed no later than July 6.

Display: Once you have received all three packets from the other participating libraries, create a display of all of the materials. You will probably want to obtain a U.S. map so that you can show the locations of each Milford.

Figure 7.8 Send instructions to each participating library to ensure that the program runs smoothly. The active part of my program ran during June, with the displays up in July and August. Four libraries including my own participated.

Milford, [State]

Our [Town/Village/City]

[Write a short description of your town that includes things like: founding date, history, population, and points of interest (major businesses, attractions, historical or natural landmarks, etc.)]

Our Library

[Write a short description of your library that includes things like: yearly circulation, number of borrowers, collection size, and founding year. Are you an independent library or part of a system?

Our Summer

[Write a short description of summer happenings in your town and library. What major events are taking place? What programs does your library have planned? What's your summer reading program theme?]

Figure 7.9 The coordinator at each library should complete this Community Profile Template.

Figure 7.10 Display featuring the photographs and community information sent from each library. A map pinpoints the locations of each Milford. Due to space constraints, letters and pictures are assembled in the binder displayed at the lower left.

The Spreading Cheer Project

For nine years, teen patrons of Willard Memorial Library (OH) have spent the month of November making small gifts to distribute as holiday presents at area nursing homes. Inspired by her own trip to one of these facilities, Kimberly Aguilar of the library's Youth Services Department saw this project as both a great outreach and an opportunity to help local students fulfill their community service requirements. Charlotte Cunningham, Head of the Youth Services Department, says, "The nursing homes are always thrilled to get our small gifts. We know the residents enjoy our creations, because we hear from visiting relatives, or see for ourselves that the items are either sitting or hanging in their rooms...sometimes long past Christmas." This is a thoughtful program that serves three communities: teens needing service hours, the library desiring to promote its services, and the nursing home residents receiving a bit of holiday cheer.

Make It Happen

1. Begin by establishing a relationship with a local senior organization. Chances are your library already does outreach to at least one. Nursing homes are a great choice because the residents may have limited opportunities to participate in community and holiday events. Other potential partners include: assisted living facilities, senior centers, and Meals on Wheels. Find out how many seniors the organization serves so that you'll know how many gifts are needed. Willard Memorial Library partners with two nursing homes, requiring 150 gifts.

2. Choose an easy craft project that will make a nice gift. Over the years, Willard Memorial Library teens have made angel ornaments, pine cone trees, sphere ornaments out of recycled cards, and candy cane reindeer. Staff find gift ideas in craft magazines, books, and websites, and by attending craft shows. Projects that use recycled materials help cut down on expenses.

3. This program requires some advance planning, particularly if gathering recycled materials. Make sure to allow enough time to gather and prepare supplies prior to the start of the project. Willard Memorial Library has teens begin making gifts the first week of November in order to have the required quantity ready for distribution the second week of December.

4. This activity doesn't just have to be for teens. Lots of adults and older children enjoy crafting and serving others. Because of age restrictions, preteens sometimes have difficulty finding volunteer opportunities. Making these gifts is a great project for them.

5. As a way of promoting the project and ensuring that a lot of gifts are made quickly, Charlotte recommends holding a kickoff event on a Saturday afternoon. Have examples of the completed gift, prepare all of the supplies, and invite teens to attend. Staff supervision will likely be required. Once the event is over, run the gift-making project as a passive program with all of the materials and instructions set up on a table in the library. Encourage kickoff attendees to come back to make more gifts.

6. Advertise the project well in advance. Make posters (Fig. 7.11) and display samples of the gift in the library. Ask the local schools to announce this service opportunity to their students.

7. When all of the gifts have been made, attach tags to each identifying that the gift is from the library. The tag might read something like: "Happy Holidays from the [Teens or Patrons] at [Your Name] Library."

8. Coordinate with the partner organization to determine the best way to distribute the gifts. Willard Public Library drops off the gifts at the nursing home and staff there distribute them with the residents' lunch trays. Alternatives include making door-to-door visits or passing out the gifts at a seasonal party hosted at the facility.

Evaluation

There are two different sets of participation numbers that can be gathered for this program. First, there are the teens that made the gifts. Count how many different teens participated. An easy way to keep track is by asking crafters to drop off the completed gifts at the service desk. If teens are completing the project for service credit, they will probably stop by anyway to have you acknowledge their work on a form or in a letter. Second, there are the seniors who receive the gifts. Depending upon how you track statistics, these numbers might be recorded as outreach instead of programming. The number of gifts made should equal the number of participating seniors.

Collection Tie-In

When distributing the gifts, the library has a prime opportunity to promote services. What items in your collection or programs that you offer would be of particular interest to seniors? Create a large print brochure to be left with the gift. The holiday season is a good time for this sort of outreach, particularly to the homebound, as these people may have relatives visiting who can assist them in accessing the library. Possible services to promote:

- Homebound delivery

- Large-print materials

- Audio books

- eBooks

- Internet access

- Adaptive technologies

- Programs

Alternative Approaches

There are many opportunities for variations on this program. Have the community create thank-you cards to be sent to soldiers serving overseas or local members of the police and fire departments. Create gifts or decorations for another holiday, such as the 4th of July, Halloween, or Thanksgiving. What other organizations in your community might you partner with? How about a homeless shelter, women's shelter, or children's hospital?

The Clermont County Public Library (OH) has provided patrons with a variety of opportunities to support current and former service men and women. One popular activity, developed by Tracey McCullough, had participants hand making Valentines and writing notes expressing appreciation and well wishes. Hundreds of Valentines were collected and conveyed to a local organization, the Yellow Ribbon Support Center, to be distributed to members of the military (Fig. 7.12).

The Spreading Cheer Project

Calling all TEENS!

Do you need community service hours? Do you enjoy that feeling you get when you brighten someone's day? Grab a friend and join us anytime on **November 1st from 11:00AM – 3:00PM** to make special Christmas gifts for our area

nursing homes. Can't make it that day... drop in **anytime the Library is open from November 1st – December 1st** and make a gift. It's sure to be lots of fun, and the smiles you will bring to the elderly of our community will be PRICELESS!

Figure 7.11 Poster recruiting teen volunteers to make gifts to be distributed at nursing homes.

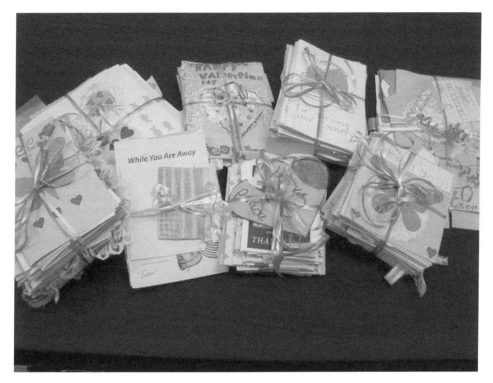

Figure 7.12 Bundles of Valentines made by Clermont County Public Library patrons, ready to be distributed to service men and women. Courtesy of Amy Prewitt.

Chapter 8

Theme Months

The two programs in this chapter provide examples of how you can take over the entire library for a month with passive programs and accompanying displays, all based around a single theme. Planning a theme month takes lots of work, so you probably won't do it very often, but it can also be a lot of fun if you can get your coworkers on board and excited. Because theme months are an undertaking, you really want to make your efforts count. Obviously any theme you pick should have wide public appeal. To narrow that field a bit, either pick a theme for which you have really good supporting materials, like my coworkers and I did for '80s Month, or pick a theme that ties in with a community event, like Celebrate Cicadas did.

The Make It Happen sections of each program write-up in this chapter vary slightly from those in the previous chapters. Instead of giving step-by-step instructions, I give you brief descriptions of a variety of activities that fit each theme. Combine several of these activities and you'll be well on your way to transforming your library for the month. Celebrate Cicadas and 80s Month won't be feasible for every library, so instead, think of these programs as inspirational models. Pick a theme that you and your coworkers can get behind, and then have fun planning a month's worth of displays and activities.

80s Month

One of the most fun projects I've participated in with my coworkers was a month-long celebration of the 1980s decade. We transformed the library with 1980s artifacts, displays, trivia contests, historical tidbits, and more. A similar effort could be undertaken with any decade. Maybe your library or city has a major anniversary coming up and you can spotlight the decade of its founding. If you pick a time period when many of your coworkers were alive, you should have good success tapping both their collective memories and basements for ideas and decorations. If you feature an earlier decade, this would be a good time to partner with your local historical society, which can likely offer resources. Much of the under-45, over-25 crowd has a soft spot for the 1980s, so this program is a way to grab their attention.

Two of my fellow coworkers, Kelly Clark and Katy Dettinger, were major contributors in developing the following 80s Month activities, but everyone at the Milford-Miami Township Branch of Clermont County Public Library (OH) deserves a nod for their willingness to help pull the event together.

Make It Happen

Banner—If you're old enough to remember dot matrix printers, then you might also remember celebrating birthdays and other special occasions with a banner printed on continuous-feed paper. Do you also remember using markers to painstakingly hand color each of the letters for extra pizzazz? Make your 1980s tribute clear to library visitors by hanging a banner in the entrance. Ours had smiley faces and read: "Totally Awesome 80s Month." If you're working with Microsoft Word, you can get large letters using a boxy font such as Arial Black and employing the outline font function. Use a huge font size and print in landscape. If you don't have a printer that handles continuous-feed paper, glue the separate sheets together after printing. Don't forget the markers! Rainbow letters will only enhance the effect (Fig. 8.1).

80s Artifacts Display—Most libraries have display cases. Recruit coworkers and friends to bring in 1980s-era items from home and create an eclectic display, perfect to prompt reminiscing. My library was able to fill two large cases with toys, movies, albums, books, magazines, computer hardware and software, jewelry, clothing, and more. Fill your display case to the brim and it will likely be your most popular 80s Month feature (Fig. 8.2).

80s History—Add an educational element to the month by spotlighting 1980s history and culture. Shelving end panels are a great place to display such information. Create a timeline of major events and, depending upon space, feature one or two years on each panel. In addition to event lists, we also made posters titled "Class of 198x," which showed pictures of people prominent in those years (Fig. 8.3).

80s Trivia—Throughout the month, offer a different trivia contest each week. We created two multiple-choice quizzes. One quiz covered 1980s politics and current events, while the other asked questions about period movies, music, and television. The other two contests were called Name That Band and Name That Movie. Movie stills or band photos were displayed and participants were challenged to identify the images. Offer 1980s-themed prizes such as a greatest hits CD or a DVD of one of the decade's popular movies.

Celebrity Crushes—Invite patrons to confess their 1980s celebrity crushes. Find out if they carried a torch for Molly Ringwald or Michael J. Fox. Cover a piece of foam board with colorful paper. Add some heart stickers and love-themed doodles. Use notebook paper and markers to create a sign asking, "Who was your celebrity crush?" Supply slips of paper and pencils for responses. Use thumbtacks to pin the submissions to the foam board (Fig. 8.4).

Slang Bookmarks—Send library visitors home with a fun souvenir. Create a list of family-friendly slang terms from the 1980s such as *bodacious, chill pill, goober, heinous,* and *stellar*. Type the terms like dictionary entries, with definitions and examples of the words used in sentences. Format the entries so that they can be printed out on colorful paper and cut into bookmarks.

Staff Photos—Try and talk your coworkers into supplying pictures of themselves from the 1980s. The bigger the hair and the louder the clothes, the better! If you can get enough photographs, make a poster with all of the pictures and see if your patrons can identify who's who. We titled our poster "Your Totally Awesome Milford-Miami Staff."

Evaluation

Overall participation in an event like 80s Month is hard to gauge, because everyone who enters the building likely takes in at least a few of the displays. To determine how many people actively interacted with the theme, count the number of entries from each trivia contest, the number of celebrity crushes submitted, and even the number of bookmarks distributed.

Collection Tie-In

- Bestsellers of the 1980s

- Nonfiction materials about the 1980s

- Music from the 1980s

- Movies from the 1980s

- Television shows from the 1980s—If your selection is limited, consider posting a list of 1980s shows owned in your library system and encourage patrons to place holds.

Resources

CBS News, "The 1980s Interactive Timeline," http://www.cbsnews.com/elements/2008/11/12/earlyshow/time line4596685.shtml (cited July 22, 2011). Timeline of major events from the 1980s.

Hawes Publications, "Adult *New York Times* Best Seller Listings," http://www.hawes.com/pastlist.htm (cited July 22, 2011). Historical *New York Times* best seller lists by year.

In the 80s, http://www.inthe80s.com/ (cited July 22, 2011). Music, movies, TV, fads, fashion, slang, and events of the 1980s.

Like Totally 80s, http://www.liketotally80s.com (cited July 22, 2011). Music, TV, movies, culture, fashion, and party planning ideas of the 1980s.

Figure 8.1 Banner welcoming library visitors to 80s Month.

Figure 8.2 Display cases full of 1980s artifacts.

Figure 8.3 End panel display of 1980s history and prominent figures.

Figure 8.4 Celebrity Crushes activity.

Celebrate Cicadas

Like many other places across the eastern United States, every 17 years, my region plays host to millions of periodical cicadas. For those who have never experienced it, a cicada emergence is a phenomenon never to be forgotten. For a few short weeks, these large, harmless insects are everywhere, their song filling the air. At this time, the newspaper is full of stories about cicadas, and everyone is talking about cicadas, so it only makes sense for the library to embrace the topic too. Plan a month of cicada-themed activities to coincide with the emergence of your local brood, and educate your patrons about these infrequent visitors.

Organizing a theme month takes a good deal of planning, but it can also be a lot of fun, especially when enthusiastic coworkers are involved. The staff of the Milford-Miami Township Branch of Clermont County Public Library (OH) helped refine each of these activities and lent their artistic talents to the undertaking.

Make It Happen

Cicada Display—Introduce the month's theme with a display of cicada-related materials. Post interesting trivia, information on morphology and habits, a timeline of what to expect during the emergence period, and photographs. Try to find news articles on past emergences in your area and add them to the display. Set up Cicada Stations around the library, each with a different activity. Create a Cicada Station logo and post it at each spot. Feature the logo prominently in your display, post a list of the month's activities, and encourage visitors to participate in each (Fig. 8.5–Fig. 8.6).

The Indoor Invasion—Our youngest patrons are always eager for a coloring sheet. Make up coloring pages with the outline of a cicada and set out the crayons. Create an indoor invasion of cicadas by hanging up the completed coloring sheets all around the library. If time allows, encourage children to bring their pictures directly to a staff member and help the child decide where to hang the drawing.

Origami Cicadas—Patterns to make origami cicadas are readily available online and in origami books. Provide instructions, possibly at a table in the library's teen area, and put out origami paper (Fig. 8.7).

Cicada Memories—Since they emerge once every 17 years, only adults will be old enough to remember previous cicada appearances in your community. Invite adults to write about their memories and allow them to be posted in the library for others to read. Create a cicada memories recording form with blank lines for writing (Fig. 8.8).

Find the Cicadas—Make giant cicadas and hide them around the library. This is easily done using large pieces of paper cut into squares and folded following an origami pattern. At the Cicada Station, be sure to post an example, since the library will be filled with many different cicada images. Make it known how many cicadas are hidden, and tell participants to come to the desk when all have been found. Offer a small prize, such as candy or bookmarks. Make a cheat sheet for employees listing all of the hiding places.

Evaluation

Track participation at each Cicada Station and add those numbers together for total involvement in the month's events. Track how many pieces of origami paper and coloring sheets are put out, how many cicada memories are turned in, and how many prizes are given out to scavenger hunt participants.

Alternative Approaches

What if your community doesn't have the pleasure of periodical cicadas? Your town probably has associations with some other animal. Maybe you host an annual lobster fest, maybe an endangered species frequents your area, maybe the high school mascot is a lion, or maybe the local zoo has just begun exhibiting komodo dragons. Any of these scenarios provide an opportunity to host a similar month of events. Simply modify the activities accordingly, or dream up some alternatives.

Resources

Books

Kritsky, Gene. *In Ohio's Backyard: Periodical Cicadas.* Columbus: Ohio Biological Survey, 1999.

Kritsky, Gene. *Periodical Cicadas: The Plague and the Puzzle.* Indianapolis: Indiana Academy of Science, 2004.

Websites

Cicada Mania, http://www.cicadamania.com (cited July 22, 2011). Extensive information on cicadas, including photographs, sounds, and videos. Find a coloring sheet and a template to make cicada stickers.

College of Mount St. Joseph, "The Mount's Cicada Web Site," http://inside.msj.edu/academics/faculty/kritskg/cicada/Site/Cicada_home.html (cited July 22, 2011). Information about emerging broods of periodical cicadas, which include maps and calendars, cicada facts, and teaching resources. Under Teaching Resources, find a cicada coloring sheet and instructions to make origami cicadas.

Look around the library for these Cicada Station signs.   There is a different activity for you to do at each spot!

Color a cicada!
Learn about cicadas!
Make an origami cicada!
Hunt for hidden cicadas!
Share your cicada memories!

Figure 8.5 Poster introducing the Cicada Stations logo.

Cicada Station

The Indoor Invasion: Decorate a Cicada

Decorate one of these cicadas and leave it in the tray. We'll hang your cicada up in the library so that it can be part of The Indoor Invasion!

Figure 8.6 Example of a Cicada Station sign.

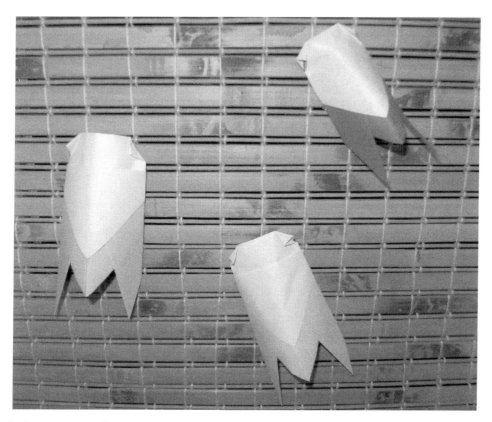

Figure 8.7 Origami cicadas.

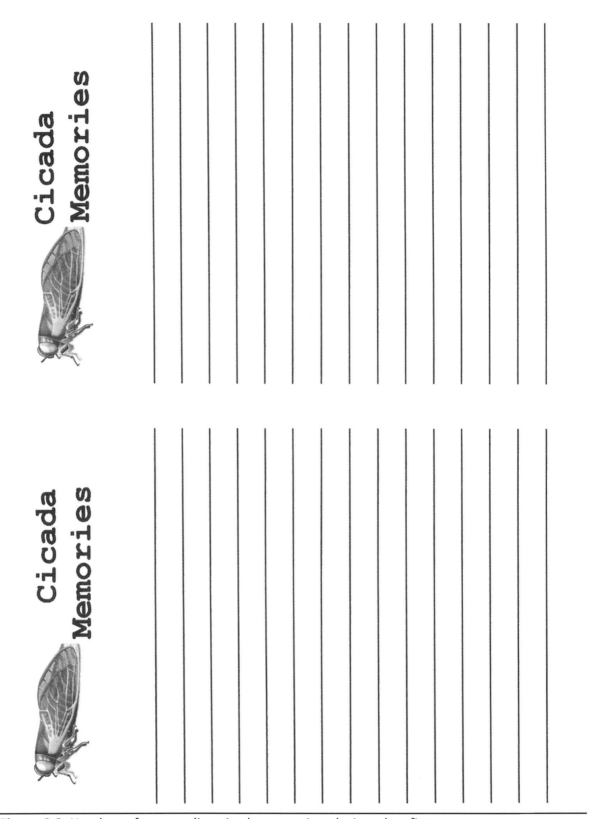

Figure 8.8 Handouts for recording cicada memories, designed to fit two per page.

Index

About the Author

EMILY T. WICHMAN has a B.S. in biological aspects of conservation and history of science, in addition to a M.A. in library and information studies, all from the University of Wisconsin–Madison. She is branch supervisor and adult services librarian at the Milford-Miami Township Branch of Clermont County Public Library in Milford, OH. She has worked for the library since 2003.

Made in the USA
San Bernardino, CA
17 March 2014